Also, by Kenneth J. Kohutek

Children's Cognitive Enhancement Program: Combined Levels
Revised Edition (with Ann M. Kohutek)

Children's Cognitive Enhancement Program
Yellow Book: Combined Levels
Revised Edition (with Ann M. Kohutek)

Chloe and Josh Learn Grit and Resilience
with Grit Gal: Volume 1

Nina Y Santi Aprenden Determinación Y Resiliencia Con La
Amiguita Determinación: Volumen I
(Translated by Flavia Merschmann)

Grit Gal Teaches Social-Emotional Skills: Volume 2

They Called Me
"DOC OF THE NEW ALCATRAZ"

Memories from the United States Penitentiary
at Marion, Illinois

KENNETH KOHUTEK, PH.D.

BALBOA.PRESS

A DIVISION OF HAY HOUSE

Balboa Press books may be ordered through booksellers or by contacting:

Balboa Press
A Division of Hay House
1663 Liberty Drive
Bloomington, IN 47403
www.balboapress.com
844-682-1282

Print information available on the last page.

ISBN: 979-8-7652-5144-7 (sc)
ISBN: 979-8-7652-5148-5 (hc)
ISBN: 979-8-7652-5147-8 (e)

Library of Congress Control Number: 2024908071

Balboa Press rev. date: 04/19/2024

CONTENTS

CONTENTS

DEDICATION

This book is dedicated to:

MY PARENTS

STAFF AND INMATES AT MARION DURING
THE YEARS I WAS PART OF THE MILIEU

CORRECTIONAL OFFICERS AND
THOSE WHO ENFORCE THE LAW

PREFACE

It was 1963 and many were celebrating the Kennedy years of 'Camelot'. While U.S. troops were already in Vietnam, most Americans could not locate the continent, much less pinpoint the country, on a map. We survived the Bay of Pigs fiasco and the Cuban Missile Crisis. The country was deeply involved in the cold war against the Soviet Union and the spread of communism. During those years, few paid attention to the closing of the landmark on an island in San Francisco Bay. The infamous Alcatraz closed its doors as a federal penitentiary for the last time.

A train loaded with inmates and inventory items, including a dental chair, traveled halfway across the country to a small town in southern Illinois. It was there, outside the community of Marion, a new prison was open. The facility, United States Penitentiary--Marion, Illinois (USP-Marion), became the maximum-security facility for the Bureau of Prisons. For several years it served as the 'new' Alcatraz until it was replaced by the United States Penitentiary Maximum Facility (ADX) in Florence, Colorado in 1994.

I was employed at USP-Marion for six years (1977-1982) when it was the maximum-security penitentiary. The experiences I describe are not meant to be the overall scope, or big picture, of events occurring during the time covered in these writings. Instead, they are from forty-five-year-old memories of a young professional responding to events occurring in his life. In hindsight, there are things I would have done differently.

I left the safety of a minimum-security facility near Dallas, Texas, and drove to a state I had not imagined visiting, much less making my residence. Always ready for a challenge, my wife and I packed the small U-Haul trailer of belongings and headed north. We were not only going to THE maximum-security federal prison, but the blizzard of 1978 was more than helpful in teaching me how to shovel snow.

The opportunity to share this part of our society was one I was glad to have experienced, but not one I want to revisit. While writing these memories, I would wonder why I did not complete my twenty years of service and be on a nice retirement plan. At various times, memories resurrected the cumulation of stress. The 'gloominess' led to a less-than-healthy environment for me was enough to recall the reasons for leaving what started as a promising career.

After transferring to the Federal Reformatory in Petersburg, Virginia, the mental health professionals provided a provisional diagnosis of Post-Traumatic Stress Disorder (PTSD) for me. When an individual in the business office and I exchanged words concerning a question about my per diem, I gathered my belongings and began to walk out of the prison. My plan was to return to Illinois and Marion when the chief of psychology caught me to resolve the situation. After a lengthy discussion, I agreed to stay and perform my duties. After sharing the experience with my fellow psychologists, it was suggested I not leave the psychology area without an escort. They expressed concern about me picking a fight with a correctional officer. I am sure they were smiling and joking, but I heeded their request. In case you miss the humor in their concern, correctional officers traditionally were considered big, bad, and mean, while psychologists were viewed as cupcakes.

I recall doing things which would be considered inappropriate, disrespectful, or demonstrating poor judgment.

A contributing factor to my positive adjustment at the Petersburg prison was my office being in the segregation unit. I was comfortable in my assignment because I had spent four years working mostly in segregation units on my last assignment. My comfort in such an environment was the reason I was instructed to spend at least a month in the psychology department before reporting to my duty station. While not happy with the request, I became comfortable with my peers, familiar with the campus, as well as being around staff in the dining area and other places to gather. Neither of which would have happened had I been working in the Special Management Unit (SMU). SMU was housed in the Richmond building which I coined the Richmond Facility, thus making me a member of the SMURF team.

INTRODUCTION

Prepare yourself for a written tour of the penitentiary where the author worked for six years. During the tour, we will visit the therapeutic community, which was closed during my internship year, segregation units, Control Unit, camp, hospital, and the corridor on which five of the eight cell blocks opened. I will introduce several inmates, administrators, and correctional staff. All names were changed to protect them and their family's privacy.

These chapters will provide a glimpse of what was a life-changing experience. There were those who successfully spent more time working in this or similar situations. However, I was unprepared for what was behind the grills leading to the corridors from which these stories originated. I was too young or naive to stay longer. I am blessed to have had the opportunity to experience firsthand what most people only view on television, the internet, or read about in books.

Get your favorite beverage, kick back in a comfortable chair, and enjoy the tour.

CHAPTER 1

WELCOME TO MARION

Kung Fu

"If you come back tomorrow, you'll be my punk", were the first words I heard from an inmate at the United States Penitentiary near Marion, Illinois. He was six foot, two inches tall and obviously spent time in the weight shack. He was disheveled, with matted hair and small pieces of cotton distributed throughout his dark hair, wore a military fatigue jacket, and jump boots. The boot laces were untied, with the tongue overlapping the laces. As an officer in the United States Army on Academic Delay, I had seen and worn a similar uniform, but surprised to see parts of military garb worn in the fashion he was wearing them. Further, I was not accustomed to a greeting like the one which started our conversation.

This first conversation behind the grills made me more curious than intimidated or alarmed. I explained I was in my internship year in a psychology doctoral program and needed to complete fifty weeks or two thousand hours of training. I assured him I was not returning to the university without documentation of completing the training. I asked his name to which he replied, "Kung Fu." I assured Kung Fu I would return in the morning.

I gathered Kung Fu (probably not his given name) decided not to make me his punk but to talk instead. He was vague or did not answer questions regarding his personal life, such as where he was reared, the crime for which he was found guilty, or how long he had been in this penitentiary. He asked if I worked for the FBI because I asked so many questions. I reminded him I was studying to be a psychologist, and asking questions was a way of getting to know someone.

His curiosity waned because, after a few days, he stopped coming by. When I saw him in the hall and spoke, he ignored my greetings and acted as if he did not know me. He demonstrated the attitude of many prisoners I saw in the corridors. Many of those incarcerated seemed determined not to acknowledge and avoid staff when the population was moving through the corridors. He was not only the first inmate I met, but the first diagnosed with Schizophrenic Reaction, paranoid type.

My office was down a corridor with a metal door leading to the main corridor of the prison. The door remained unlocked and open during my first days. Initially, inmates who participated in educational classes or requesting reading material would walk by. The education department relocated to the area previously occupied by the community which left the psychology department, me at the time, the only department housed in the corridor. An administrator recommended I keep the door locked and opened only when an inmate was to meet with me. The new chief mandated leaving the door shut and locked which limited access to psychologists. Either decision left the department safe but isolated and prevented access to the department.

I found the availability of the units positive but, at the same time, vulnerable to possible volatile situations.

The Chief of Psychology

Between chats with Kung Fu, I had books to read before meeting with my supervisor. After perusing the stack of literature, we met. Dr. B was shorter and more softly spoken than one might expect. His smiling disposition was incongruent with his blunt, often rude, honesty. During our initial session, Dr. B. informed me I was not his first choice as an intern. Nevertheless, he agreed to supervise me. He commented my assignment had been based on being friends with someone in the Central Office. Even though the Director of Psychological Services in the Central Office had previously provided supervision, I felt the need to assure him this internship was not the most desired placement. However, it was important to remain a student to satisfy the internship year, so I kept my thoughts to myself.

After Dr. B.'s tour in the Air Force, the Department of Public Health hired him. His employment with the department meant, while working in the prisons, the agency could reassign him to other bureaus, such as the Bureau of Indian Affairs. He explained the reason for being at this facility was the therapeutic community. He shared the history and his perceptions of the program in a tone of reverence one may have in telling an intimate story about one's family or repeating a story from a religious doctrine.

In 1968, USP-Marion hired Martin Groder, M.D. He had spent the previous three years completing his psychiatric training at the University of California-San Francisco. Eric Berne, M.D., and a member of Berne's San Francisco Social Psychiatric Seminar mentored him. The seminar members developed the Transactional Analysis (TA) framework, which Berne later published. The goal of TA was to assist patients in understanding their transactions and how those transactions enhance or interfere with relationships.

Dr. Groder started a therapeutic community in 1969 called

'Asklepieon.' The community was based on two modalities popular in California during those years. Synanon, started by Charles Dederick, a licensed hypnotherapist and member of AA, developed the program for individuals with addictions. The part of Synanon borrowed for the Marion program was the "Game," a form of attack therapy (more later in this chapter). The Game broke down defenses one might have in preventing cognitive changes. The second modality was Transactional Analysis (TA) which provided feedback and information on ways to develop healthier thinking and relationships.

Dr. Groder stayed with the program until 1972, when he became the warden of the Federal Center for Correctional Research Butner, North Carolina. The program he started lasted until there was a movement underway to do away with most programs in the prison system.

The program invited volunteers from the general population with the only promised benefit being the potential of remaining out of illegal behavior and avoiding future arrests. If the volunteers involved themselves in the program and received no institutional infractions for two years, the psychologist would write a letter to the parole board documenting participation. This type of endorsement was favorable but did not assure a positive outcome with a parole board hearing. In some situations, the positive report was not beneficial because of events occurring before or during incarceration.

Attending my first Community Meeting

The community schedule started with the 8:00 a.m. meeting. My supervisor expected me to be part of the community as well as a member of the professional team. On my second day, a participant asked me the reason I had not talked during the

4

two meetings I had already attended. He accused me of being an "uppity, white college boy" who thought I was too good to participate. A second member joined in, followed by all members yelling at me about my attitude and nonparticipation. Having been the victim of one was how I learned the meaning of 'rat pack' in the Synanon game. The confrontation ended with the member who started the 'rat pack' requested I involve myself in the community because of benefits the group could experience based on my training.

After the group, I returned to my office, slumped in my chair, and looked at the grey wall across the desk. Reviewing the first week of my internship, I experienced the welcome/warning from Kung Fu, the chief's less than enthusiastic welcome, and the confrontation in the group, then said to no one, "Welcome to Marion!" I survived week one! Only fifty-one weeks left in my internship.

CHAPTER 2

THE THERAPEUTIC COMMUNITY

Who are you?

The second week started, and I hoped it would be more of a positive experience. Having met Kung Fu, learning my supervisor was not overwhelmed with my placement, and the confrontation in the community was as traumatic as some experiences in graduate school. Fortunately, the events of the following weeks and months were less traumatic. Another explanation for the lowered stress level was I became acclimated to the environment and less intimidated.

Adjusting and settling into this workplace would prove to be more difficult than other settings. Unlike other jobs, neither the chief nor staff psychologist introduced me to line staff or any inmates. I was an anomaly to those I would be spending most of the internship and following years unknown to most. The glances I got from both staff and inmates were understandable. All were trying to figure out who the 'new guy' was. Fortunately, I had a name tag and could identify myself when quarried. Being new with no one aware of me or my functions, I decided it was my responsibility to ensure my name be known through the cell blocks.

The first correctional officer I met called me 'Doc.' I tried to explain I had not completed the requirements to have the handle. Nevertheless, the title caught on; none of my professors were around to correct them, and the handle was easier to pronounce than my surname, so I went with it. As time progressed, being called "Doc" was comforting after hearing the names given to me as I made my way through the segregation units.

With the assistance of Dr. B., I developed a schedule and settled into the role of a psychology intern. Mornings started in the community where the Program Director, Chief Psychologist, two senior member inmates, and I would review the day's schedule.

After my first confrontation, the 8:00 a.m. "Game" was less traumatic. After thinking about the confrontation and feedback, I recalled having attended college for years, worked at a county mental health unit for three years, as well as at the Federal Correctional Institution in Seagoville, Texas for a year. This was a new setting, but I was sure those experiences prepared me for this challenge. I began to climb out of my introverted shell and become a member of a challenging workplace.

During the second hour, community members were divided into three groups. The division was based on their knowledge of TA. I read and was familiar with the concepts, but this experience deepened my knowledge and skills in using the jargon and therapeutic impact.

As a newcomer, I was placed in the level covering basic concepts. An introduction to TA, history of TA, ego states, and examples of transactions were taught. Some members would get confused while discussing the different ego states and, consequently, spent more time than others in this basic group. Once a member could discuss the basics of TA, he would be moved to the second level.

The second level explored transactions, games, and scripts. Participants were encouraged to examine the comparison of transactions before incarceration, identifying transactions over the course of their day, as well as examining how future transactions could be used for healthier, more genuine relationships. This level of instruction was crucial because transactions in which most members engaged in prior to incarceration were manipulative and often resulting in legal and interpersonal difficulties. Empathy was introduced because not being able to consider the perspective of others was common. While most members could 'read' people, the information was used to manipulate rather than relate to a person.

Most members had difficulty identifying their feelings. Once the realization of feelings occurred, finding the words, and expressing those feelings to others was a struggle. From an early age, most had been conditioned to realize they were vulnerable when expressing feelings. The anxiety level was obvious when encouraged to share feelings in a group. By conducting groups at the mental health unit, child protective services, and the university counseling center, I learned the difficulty nonincarcerated clients had in sharing thoughts and feelings. The difficulty was exponential in this setting where expressing feelings were often life threating.

The advanced level included a combination of the previous levels and reviewing life scripts in greater detail, crooked transactions, and transactions happening daily. This group was the one in which the most time was spent. It was beneficial because of the time given participants to understand and apply knowledge gained in the previous classes.

The third group was intended to be fun and less intense. Fun and relaxing if the members knew the answers to questions about TA, were developing a sense of humor, and learning not to take themselves as seriously as the persona developed in prison. Feeling comfortable in their "own skin" was not a strength of most members. The usual mindset was unrealistic self-perceptions, threatened by feedback incongruent with their belief system. Defensiveness, anger, and aggression were implemented to defend their reality.

The group started with the leader asking TA questions. A group member was 'randomly' selected to give the correct answer. I stressed the word 'randomly' because I was positive my name was called more often than others. Consequences for incorrect answers varied but involved the person engaging in some 'off-the-wall behavior.' An example of a consequence was standing facing the group and singing "I'm a little teapot" with hand gestures. There was something humorous about watching 'hardened' criminals (and a young intern) being able to laugh and not take oneself seriously. The seasoned members were not as easily offended when dealing with a consequence than the newcomers. Also, their knowledge had grown, resulting in fewer consequences. This group was an opportunity for the Child's ego state to play as well as serve a motivator to master TA concepts. Newcomers had difficulty at times because smiling, laughing, and not taking oneself seriously were foreign to those having served time in prisons.

The morning activities ended with time to read or discuss the material presented earlier in the day. The class after lunch was 'Mental Health' and facilitated by the psychologist. Topics included depression, addiction, perspective-taking, and stress management. The remainder of the day was for individual therapy sessions. The schedule was organized in a manner allowing each resident at least two weekly sessions with the psychologist. Those not scheduled to have a session had responsibilities in the unit or elsewhere in the facility. The schedule exposed participants to hundreds of therapy hours.

The Honor System

Community members lived in the same unit. If there were backsliding or infractions of unit or institution guidelines, it would be obvious to at least one member. It became the responsibility of the witness to discuss the infraction during the next 8:00 a.m. group. If a member observed the breaking of a rule by another resident and did not mention the concern, the person observing the infraction could find himself on the hot seat. Included in the discussion would be his not following unit rules or not caring about the progress of other members of the community.

This requirement was opposite of the universal rule found in prisons. The unwritten rule, 'say nothin' to nobody' was usually enforced with death. The first time an inmate was confronted in the 8:00 am group, anger would be directed toward the one mentioning the infraction. At some point, the word 'snitch' would be used with posturing and walking toward the member who initiated the confrontation. There was no violence, with the new member being reminded the feedback was to assist in the growth process and not meant to be destructive, threatening, or result in an Incident Report.

If the community was 'clean' with participants engaged in recovery, the "Game" was productive. On the other hand, if there were covert contracts between residents, some members were confronted, and others were not. The covert contracts were intensively studied by guests visiting and monitoring the program. As indicated by its name, a covert contract is when two or more individuals agree to work outside the rules to protect one another.

This concern will be further addressed in the Thoughts section.

National Notoriety

The program was nationally recognized, with facilities nationwide studying and modeling the community. As a result of the notoriety, visitors interested in developing similar programs in a prison or treatment center were frequent observers. The Florida Correctional System, for example, was impressed with the program and often sent staff from different facilities to observe, return, and replicate the model. State agencies often hired participants from the program who were soon to be paroled. Motivation of newer members increased after seeing senior members receiving parole dates and/or hired because of the knowledge gained from participating in the program.

Other visitors included consultants specializing in therapeutic communities and TA. Their goal was to assess the effectiveness of the program with suggestions being implemented. Most feedback was directed to keeping the milieu 'clean' and functioning at its highest level. The feedback was valuable with 'drift' often not noticed by staff involved daily in the program. Becoming involved in covert contracts as well as the halo effect had to be closely monitored.

CHAPTER 3

THE DEATH OF A PROGRAM

Concerns Regarding the Program

Despite the program being nationally recognized, bureau administrators on several levels were concerned about its cost-effectiveness and efficacy. Maintaining Marion's security level was a major expense; the ratio of staff involved in the rehabilitation program compared to staff working in the general population was disproportional. The program used more staff per inmate than the general population. It was argued housing inmates at Marion not needing the level of security did not make financial sense. An example of the drain on manpower could be found in the psychology department. The Chief Psychologist committed his entire time to the community, while the other psychologist shouldered the responsibilities of the rest of the prison population.

Another concern went to the heart of the program's mission. How effective was the program in bringing about a permanent behavioral change? Correctional programs use the rate of recidivism as a measure of success. Considering the lengthy sentences of most participants, recidivism would not be a realistic measure of efficacy. What variables could measure success in the therapeutic community? While I am sure there were success stories, there were also incidents of no improvement. Reader beware! The fact I saw no hard data did not mean data was not available.

Another concern was the possibility of teaching participants to be 'better' criminals. Critics argued the program was counterproductive. Once learning the rules of the "Game" and memorizing TA terms, one with an antisocial personality could adapt, present as improving, but not have experienced permanent cognitive changes. How could one with a lengthy criminal lifestyle be trusted when expressing interest in the program? How could the behavioral and cognitive change be assessed before sending the participant to a less secure facility or paroled to the community? The skeptic would argue, if trying to reach a goal of parole or transfer, all one had to do was learn the terminology and follow the rules for twenty-four months. A strength of those with the diagnosis of antisocial personality disorder is the ability to adapt to meet their needs.

The critic would argue there were a myriad of opportunities for programs before reaching the maximum-security penitentiary. Any person aware of available programs know there are options before prison or reaching this needed level of security.

A Game Changer

When the announcement from the Central Office reiterated the mission of the Bureau of Prisons was to detain felons found guilty of a crime and remanded to serve their sentence in custody of the prison system. Therefore, programs like the therapeutic community did not fit into the mission. The system closed the community with participating staff and inmates granted a transfer. Literature related to the program was destroyed with the physical space used for a different mission. Then it was no more.

Having become attached to the program and participants, I

was at a loss to understand what might happen next. But what is an intern to do? I was offered the opportunity to be transferred twice to a different facility. I declined both times stating it was not feasible. My wife, also a psychology graduate student had gained employment, and we were making payments on a house. Also, I was more concerned about completing the weeks of training than packing and moving again.

RIP Therapeutic Communities

Thoughts

Fresh out of college and having experienced positive outcomes while working at a mental health center, I found closing the program traumatic. The program was the last hope for its members. At the time, I wondered what possibilities there would be if more attention focused on education and training opportunities. As I gained experience, I realized the plethora of opportunities offered before and during incarceration were available. Therefore, I did not question the closing of the community as much as in my earlier years. Also, the populations served between a county mental health unit and Marion differed. It was difficult to have an opinion about success of therapeutic interventions in prisons when one knows little about the outcomes. While the data indicated a poor prognosis of intervention when dealing with incarcerated individuals requiring this level of security, I believed authors of previous studies arguing against the efficacy of programs at this level did not have the commitment or tenacity to persevere in therapeutic attempts.

Moving forward, based on my experiences, I gravitated toward working with younger populations. From Marion, I transferred to a federal reformatory for young adult males. Later I was the clinical director at two residential treatment centers and provided psychological services to several school districts. Seeing what might lay ahead for some difficult students motivated me to work diligently to provide a healthy foundation for all young people.

Much of the state and federal budget is spent on law enforcement, including prisons. The amount allotted annually to prisons would classify prisons as big business. A prison is often a mainstay for many communities, while other communities lobby to get a prison to boost their economy. Questions I had included:

1) How would the budgets of states and federal government differ if prisons deterred future criminal activity?
2) How would those changes in the budget impact the communities in which prisons are located?
3) How can corporations view incarcerating fellow human beings as a profit-making proposition?
4) What level of training and understanding of human nature do applicants have when prisons are placed in high-unemployment communities?

I questioned the efficacy of the therapeutic community. The program was based on two popular theories with no data supporting positive outcomes for incarcerated felons with severe personality disorders. As an aside, administration at my next placement encouraged me to develop a similar program in my assigned unit. As I introduced the model, mostly by example, those who learned the process the fastest were young offenders who most employees would describe as being the most manipulative as well as most likely to be incarcerated in the future.

Finally, with the severity and prognosis of the those incarcerated in a maximum-security prison, a positive outcome of 'talk' therapy would be dubious. Theories on which the program was based would be labeled as reeducative. Similar therapeutic approaches assume presenting information to an individual would result in behavioral change.

Individuals with personality disorders in a penitentiary would more likely respond to a deeper approach to therapy. However, reconstructive therapy is expensive and time-consuming as well as usually not receptive to those with the diagnosis.

CHAPTER 4

LIFE IN THE CELL BLOCKS

Reasons to Visit a Psychologist

After the community closed, I spent time in both the general population and segregation units. Six of the nine cell blocks opened into the same corridor as the metal door leading to my office. Because I spent time in the main corridor, I became known and received requests to meet with individuals. There were three reasons someone came to my office: curiosity, testing to see if I could be a mule, or having someone with whom to talk without accused of snitching.

The curious were window shoppers and 'just looking.' A fresh staff member, not a correctional officer, who wore a tie, with an office behind the grills was a rarity. Like those of us not incarcerated, there is curiosity about something different. Novelty, even a psychology intern, was a change in scenery. If I asked if I could help, men in this group would answer "No," or just walk away.

Others came for a less honorable reason; they wanted to determine if I could be used as a mule. A mule is exactly what it sounds like; one who would either bring contraband into or out of the facility. Examples of smuggled contraband into the prison included drugs, cash, or equipment to assist in an escape. Contraband leaving the facility would include letters not to be reviewed by correctional staff. Most staff members involved in this illegal behavior were seeking monetary gain. Other staff had gotten involved because of extortion. This sounds naïve, but to my knowledge, I did not know any mules in the facility. On the other hand, a good mule would never trust a fresh staff member.

Others came to assess my intentions. I got the impression they wanted to determine if I was a 'cop' wearing a tie or genuinely concerned about mental health. This group would come in more than once. Initially, the conversation would be superficial, including their city of origin, length of sentence, what charges led to incarceration, the St. Louis Cardinals or Chicago Cubs baseball teams.

Another question which needed to be resolved before talking to a psychologist, was the unwritten rule talking to staff was discouraged and considered to be 'snitching.' The level of distrust kept the facility on a low boil resulting in a constant state of vigilance. Like a match in a dry field, a fire, or murder/riot in this situation, could break out at any time. One reason for this lack of trust was no one knew the intentions of others. The volatility was what happened when having placed three hundred men, most of whom have been diagnosed with an antisocial personality disorder in one setting. Snitching had a high price which led to death if suspected. On the other hand, staff never discouraged sharing information. In fact, one of the surest ways to be transferred was to share information related to a planned escape, the likelihood of a confrontation between rival gangs, or where the hootch was being brewed for the Fourth of July weekend.

Joe

Other than Kung Fu, the first individual to visit more than once was Joe. Before coming in, Joe would follow the psychology consultant and me from a distance as we walked the corridors. Finally, he broke his silence, entered my office, and became one of the more frequent visitors. He was approximately five foot and eleven inches tall, overweight, and in his early forties. I attributed the weight to his not exercising and the high carbohydrate diet. He became more relaxed as we discussed his girlfriend, living in Chicago, and the rush from holding up banks. The conversation then turned to how impressed he was by the confidentiality aspect of my profession. He compared the confidentiality of psychologists to one of the unwritten rules in prisons – 'do not tell anyone anything.'

Joe explained, while a bank robber, he was not guilty of holding up the savings and loan for which he was convicted. During the trial, he could not present his defense because it would implicate him in robbing a bank across town at the same time the savings and loans was robbed. He agreed to return the amount of cash taken from the savings and loan, leaving him with the bulk of the money from the bank heist. The courts sentenced him to twenty-five years but, because he returned the money and with anticipated good behavior, would be paroled in eight years. He did not tell me how much money was taken from the bank but assured me if the funds were divided by the eight years of incarceration, his yearly income from the one robbery would make my salary look pathetic.

After describing how lucrative his career as a bank robber was, as well as his respect for confidentiality, he began talking about his crew. He started by explaining 'his' woman had been with him for years and was trustworthy. In fact, she was holding his share of the money. The guy going into the bank with him was weird because he would have an orgasm after running into the bank and watching everyone lying on the floor. We agreed he enjoyed power.

His concern was the partner who drove the getaway car. After the robbery, the driver usually got drunk, flashed a pocketful of money, and bragged. Showboating by the drunk resulted in the eventual arrest of all involved. It seemed a customary practice to dispose of the driver in a dumpster after the crew safely made their way from the bank. Joe explained because of my confidentiality, he would feel comfortable with me as the driver. He spiced up the offer by stating he had cash to get started so I would have all the women, drugs, and alcohol I wanted. For all those benefits, my only responsibility would be to sit in a car until he and his orgasmic friend got in the vehicle. I would drive to an undisclosed area where the cash would be divided. Afterwards, each of us would be on our separate ways.

I explained it was an attractive offer, but I did not know the streets of Chicago. He added I would be familiar after they practiced. To nail the deal, Joe complimented me by saying I was too smart to carry a lunch bucket into a place like this for the rest of my life, and he was providing an opportunity to get out of daily work. I assured Joe his offer humbled me, but I did not think it would work, and I did not want him to have to shoot me. Rather than hearing me turn him down, he offered time to think. There was a great retirement plan with less hassle if we were not shot or arrested. If the authorities arrested us, we would spend a few years in a place like this, then be back in business.

When he returned the following morning, I explained neither my wife nor I thought it was a promising idea to join up with him. He exclaimed including my wife in his business was a poor decision. Continuing, he said I was full of crap and sure I would not go with him even before the offer was made. Nevertheless, he said he liked me and thought we would have fun. Oh well, I would have died from an overdose, some dreaded STD, shot by the police, or by Joe himself.

Joe did not come in for a few weeks after the proposed job opportunity was turned down. The next time I saw him, he walked into the office sad and angry. He had learned 'his' woman, who he had trusted with 'his' money, had taken off with another guy as well as taken 'his' cash. His entire release plans were gone in one phone call. Joe never smiled or seemed as jovial as before he got the news. Even though we ended up knowing one another for years, I never had the heart to tell him 'his' money belonged to the bank, and his sentencing was still favorable.

Bank robbers, from my experience, had minimal insight or concern about the victims or their safety. The goal was absconding with money but not violence. Nevertheless, there was no concern about taking human life which was collateral damage. When asked about hazards in robbing a bank, the usual response was a shrug with the comment 'the bank's money is insured.' The answer did not relate to the question, which suggested there was no regard or an understanding of the legality of their actions. Neither did he realize the seriousness of bringing a loaded weapon into a place of business or show concern about those involved because of being in the wrong place at the wrong time.

Joe's friendship matched the process of 'grooming' another to be a mule. Observing from a distance provided information about me and my goals in prison. He did not mention the offer until he developed a relationship with flattering compliments. This provided a bond because of our mutual respect for confidentiality. While I never planned to join Joe in his adventures, had I agreed, I would have been requested to join the partnership before his release. The steps, or similar steps, are described during the grooming process of a potential victim in and out of prisons.

Dog

Another regular visitor preferred being called by his nickname, 'Dog.' Dog was a Caucasian male five feet, ten inches tall, and weighing one hundred and ninety pounds. During our meetings, no unusual mannerisms or behaviors were observed. His estimated intelligence was in the low average range. Dog denied ever being treated for a psychiatric diagnosis. His Presentence Investigation (PSI) supported details Dog shared. As our meetings progressed, he became relaxed and shared aspects of his life not found in the folder. It was easy for him to laugh and joke during our meetings. He once believed the song 'Desperado' by the Eagles applied to his life. He changed his opinion and stated the song applied to me because he understood what the convicts and guards were doing in this setting but described me as one who did not fit in the prison setting.

Dog was removed from a dysfunctional family at an early age and spent his developmental years in either foster care or detention centers. There had been no consistent adult care or nurturing during his formative years. His basic needs were provided for, but he had not developed a meaningful relationship with peers or adults in his placements. The first person he bonded with was a girlfriend who became his partner.

He enjoyed talking about their experiences and smiled while telling the stories. They referred to themselves as the modern-day 'Bonnie and Clyde,' but without as many murders. They occupied their time driving through west Texas, New Mexico, and Oklahoma, holding up banks. While not naming specific banks, he openly admitted to several bank robberies. While it was easy for him to discuss the robberies, he adamantly denied the rape of a hostage. During one robbery, their initial plan did not work as anticipated resulting in the taking of hostages to gain their freedom.

As they were driving their customary escape route, the female hostage asked to stop to relieve herself. Dog escorted her behind a dune and allowed her to tend to her business. After he and his partner were arrested, he learned the female hostage accused him of raping her during the stop. He assured me, if his partner thought he had raped the woman, she would have shot and left him behind the dunes.

While an interesting story, I had several questions. It did not make sense for him to escort a female hostage while his partner watched the male. The vague answer was he would be more likely to shoot her if she tried to run. Whether or not a rape occurred, he was charged with rape, found guilty, and sentenced to serve more time.

His laissez-faire attitude toward the risks involved in walking into a bank with weapons suggested he did not register the potential of injury to people, including himself and girlfriend. Once more, I found the lack of empathy in Dog's mindset a common thread in the though process of bank robbers.

While discussing the trials, he related, after being sentenced to three consecutive life sentences in federal courts, a state court found him guilty of yet another offense and sentenced him to one-hundred-years. The sentence was to be served after being paroled from the federal time. After sentencing, Dog asked permission to address the judge, who granted the request. Dog explained his sentencing structure and the three consecutive life sentences with the one-hundred-year sentence detainer was more time than he could serve. His story ended by saying the judge leaned over the bench, looked him in the eyes, and said, "Do the best you can, son." Somehow, we found humor in the judge's response. We did not have much to laugh at during those years.

A Near Assault

During most afternoons, the recreation yard was open. Much of the area behind the fences was empty and devoted to recreational purposes. There was a track, weight shack, softball backstop, a small set of bleachers by the ball field, and tables and benches to relax and sit. A signal from the intercom would alert inmates and staff it was time to return to the units for the afternoon count.

Often, I would stand in the main corridor during the yard's closing. Administrators advised me not to be in the area because I was placing myself in a situation leading to potential harm. Correctional officers and inmates seeing me during the movement served several purposes. The most important was to have another staff in the corridor during these times. I believed more staff in the area was a reassurance to the officers as well as lowering the likelihood of violence.

Inmates who already knew me might discretely nod, and some who did not might stop to ask if I was a case manager, but most of the time, I was ignored. Even though I had spent a couple of years at the prison, unless an inmate had a psychiatric history or been in the segregation unit for more than a month, most did not know who I was.

One afternoon, I watched someone running (more like staggering) toward me, yelling obscenities. As he was about to strike me, another inmate, Maurice (more about Maurice later in this chapter), grabbed him and carried him to their block. The assailant appeared drunk, or on other chemicals, because his gait was unsteady, and his swing was in slow motion. The event occurred quickly, and, like similar events, everything returned to normal in the blink of an eye.

I was thankful Maurice got involved because his six feet and three inches tall, with the two hundred and fifty pounds of muscle on his frame came in handy. My potential assailant was five feet and eight inches tall and skinny as a bean pole. Maurice physically picked him up and carried him to their unit. The corridor was filled with men returning to their units, but none got involved as they continued the movement. The event occurred in about a minute.

While I could have suffered major physical injury, the attempted assaulter would have to deal with the consequences of being inebriated and assaulting a federal employee. Except for the expression of gratitude to the orderly, no reference to the inebriated inmate or potential assault was mentioned by staff, inmates, or me.

Keith

Keith usually had a cigarette between his right hand's second and third fingers. He had dark hair with a mustache. He was alert and oriented to his surroundings. There were no symptoms which might suggest a psychiatric disorder. He was verbal, self-confident with his actions having a purpose. Keith wore an unbuttoned vest with a t-shirt underneath the vest. He talked 'hip,' and I waited for him to use a phrase like "Cool, man" or "far out" at any time. As I write this, I can hear him say, 'Yea, well, Kenny, this is what I need.' The first two words were a discount of my previous statement, with the third addressing me with a variation of my name I never used. While I assumed the name implied a friendship, it could just as well as have been a 'one up' statement with him jockeying to control the situation.

While talking, Keith would move the arm holding the cigarette in a circular motion when making a point. His gait was relaxed as if he were strolling in his neighborhood, not a penitentiary. He had adapted and normalized his mannerisms prior to incarceration to this unusual environment. His temperament was different from bank robbers because he was more serious. I never saw him laugh, but from time to time, he smiled. Because of his demeanor, it seemed natural for me not to joke or feel totally relaxed around him. Keith presented as all business.

He requested assistance in managing his anger. When angered, he would injure or murder the person who angered him. Keith's motivation to change included being tired of incarceration and wanting to work his way out of federal custody. I agreed to work with him for three reasons: his motivation to address the issue, my concern for an unsuspecting individual who inadvertently faced his anger, and my curiosity. Most psychologists did not have the opportunity to work with similar severe cases of this diagnosis in an outpatient setting. It would be interesting to determine if the behavioral techniques described in the literature would be effective in addressing anger issues as severe as those described by Keith.

A factor to consider when working with an angry issue was the 'length of the fuse.' Length of the fuse is the time between the event evoking an anger response and the behavioral response. Keith's fuse was short! It was critical for him to become aware of situations leading to anger as well as of his autonomic reactions prior to the behavioral response. With me, he created a list of situations and places where anger would most likely occur. He added being touched was a trigger for his anger. Examples on his list of locations he might experience anger included a card game, being pushed, or touched by others. Another was him hearing a negative statement about him or his friends.

We met regularly for three years. Besides identifying situations in which he might become angry, training included the ability to monitor emotional responses leading to anger. Finally, he learned alternatives in ways to express himself. Our work together placed several 'tools' put in his mental 'toolbox.' One strategy was the 'panic button' he taped to the back wall of his cell. A tiny piece of paper colored red with a piece of tape over it may have saved lives. Besides the panic button, he learned how to monitor his reactions in locations and situations leading to anger.

Finally, his goal to move toward freedom became a reality. His unit team recommended a transfer to a less secure prison, and he would be transferred to the penitentiary at Leavenworth, Kansas. Before his departure, he shared his greatest concern was his 'claws' had been snipped, and he did not feel as violent has before. He was assured he could defend himself by using the techniques he practiced. While learning self-control, he was able to use reasoning to make a point.

The Rest of the Story

Before his transfer, Keith came to the office at an unscheduled time. He informed me he was a member of a group in which another member put out a contract on me. He continued by informing me the contract was for two cartons of cigarettes, and, choosing to let me know rather than sticking to the code, a similar contract was placed on him.

He told me about contracts placed on other prison staff. I became indignant when I learned a psychologist in the California correctional system had a contract on his life for three cartons of cigarettes! I thought a psychologist in the Federal Prison System should be worth more than any psychologist working for a state.

Keith jokingly (?) added, if the contract was for three cartons,

it would be a difficult decision between letting me know or
collecting the cigarettes. We both had a good laugh at his probable
joke. He said I was an 'all-right guy' and gave me the heads up
because others were not familiar with me.

He explained how to get the contract lifted and stressed the
importance of getting the situation corrected. It was critical to
resolve the issue quickly so neither of us would be facing the
consequences. I became aware of the urgency after he told me
the name of the individual who had put out the contract. The
resolution of the contract can be found in Chapter 6 under the
heading 'Two Cartons of Cigarettes'.

Rounds Being Fired

One drizzly, foggy Tuesday morning, while the department
heads were in the Warden's meeting, the rest of us were conducting
business as usual. I heard two rounds from a high carbine rifle
fired near the prison. I stepped into the main corridor, where
the officer at a Control Center said they needed me up front
immediately. The speed the grills opened as I made my way to
the front reminded me of the parting of the waters of the Red Sea
during the exodus. An arsenal was open, and we were handed a
12-gauge shotgun, or an M-14 rifle.

We were dropped off in pairs with a shotgun and carbine
under each tower. The hospital assistant administrator (George)
and I were under the same tower, where we aimed our weapons
toward an empty rec yard. I had quit smoking cigarettes two years
prior and foolishly thought, due to the stress, it was a suitable time
to start again. I knew George, like all who smoked, carried an
extra pack in his sock in the event of an extended shift. He was
kind enough to give me a cigarette, and there we stood, lighting
cigarettes quickly extinguished by the rain.

After thirty minutes, a lieutenant drove by and asked what we were doing. George answered with a question regarding why we were standing in the rain. With a laugh, he informed us the rounds were directed toward the prison, and we were standing on the wrong side of the tower. He pointed to the two chips in the concrete above our heads. We did our best to graciously thank him for the information, but I doubt he considered either of our comments gracious.

Eventually, we were picked up, returned our weapons, and went to our various workstations. Through the rumor mill, I learned the rounds were fired at the towers to assist in an escape attempt. After the rounds were fired, two inmates on the opposite side of the yard took a board from the bleachers, laid it across the two fences, and started the crawl over the fences and concertina wire to freedom. An officer under one of the towers saw the two and ratcheted a round in the shotgun. Ratcheting a round in the shotgun made an ominous noise which was intensified by the foggy, rainy morning. The officer then watched the two crawl backwards toward the inside of the fences. A bold plan but a failed escape.

Like other situations, once the weapons were returned, life returned to its normal pace with nothing mentioned afterward.

Maurice

Maurice was the orderly for the corridor in which my office was located. His stride made him appear fearless. He was an African American from Washington, D.C. and had served part of his sentence in the Lorton Reformatory. There was no history of mental health issues and was alert as well as his surroundings during each meeting we had. He was friendly and always had something positive to share. I do not remember him complaining or being concerned about his situation in life.

Maurice was the individual who intervened during the assault who helped both his friend and me. A tangential but relevant aspect of our acquaintance occurred in the reformatory at Petersburg, Virginia which was my next assignment. Several of these youthful offenders with whom I worked did not believe I had worked at Marion. One doubter asked me to name some of the inmates I worked with while at the penitentiary. I knew the person who asked the question was from D.C. and I named Maurice by his nickname. The doubter let everyone know I was telling the truth because Maurice was his uncle which was enough to label me 'cool' and authentic. I was accepted by those in the unit and at once treated with respect.

During a conversation between Maurice, Joe, and myself, Maurice explained he was the 'godfather' of his family. He believed most wealthy families had a relative who, at some point, engaged in illegal activities to secure the family wealth. The example he used was Joe Kennedy. He designated himself as the person in his family and worked toward his goal by robbing banks. He was unmarried, had no 'known' children, and had established trust funds for his nieces and nephews. The money he provided would allow them to leave their impoverished neighborhood, get an education, invest their funds, or however, they wished to spend their assets. He explained his illegal activities were altruistic. Joe reminded him of the type of cars he drove, the clothes he wore, and the drugs he used. While laughing, Maurice responded by saying every job had its fringe benefits. The situation was not right for me to tell him his rationalizing bank robbery was rationalization. Once more, it was interesting to hear them show no remorse for their crimes or for putting the lives of others in harm's way.

James

One of my favorite inmates was also a textbook example of one with an antisocial personality. James was a Caucasian male five-foot eleven-inches tall weighing two hundred pounds. He was friendly and able to relate to a broad variety of individuals. His intelligence was in the high average or higher level. His verbal skills were impeccable with his vocabulary which resulted in staff asking him to define the words he used in daily conversation.

He admitted having had an extensive psychiatric history, including having been declared Not Guilty by Reasons of Insanity on two occasions. Each time his symptoms were treated and abated resulting in his discharge after he was declared no longer insane. Both times he returned to criminal activity and committed similar crimes. His illegal actions put a considerable number of people in harm's way as well as gaining national notoriety. The laws were changed resulting in his illegal activity becoming a federal crime. He was subsequently tried in federal court, found guilty, and placed in the custody of the federal prison system.

James claimed to have told a fictional story to an author who drafted a book based on his story. He continued to claim the story was fictional despite there was overlap between his Presentence Investigation and events in the book.

I met James when he and another inmate came to my office after the 4:00 count. He explained a social worker in Chicago agreed to escort his daughter, living in Miami, for a visit. His counselor and case manager had left for the evening, and he wanted to make sure the schedules were coordinated for the visit.

Others other than a counselor or case manager making calls were discouraged. However, the religion department and psychology staff could make calls if the situation required. I detected a sense of urgency in his story because the visit was to occur within two days. James provided the number. I dialed it and placed the phone on speaker.

The call went to an answering machine and the call disconnected. As it turned out, it was fortunate no one answered. I could say I tried to help, and the request was referred to the proper staff making the call in the morning. This innocuous request turned into a not-so-innocuous situation as the story unfolded. To learn more, refer to Chapter 7.

CHAPTER 5

SEGREGATION UNITS

Home on the Range (s)

Psychological interviews were required every thirty days an inmate was on segregation status. The reason was to monitor symptoms related to stimulus deprivation..Symptoms I was checking for included changes in anxiety, hallucinations, bizarre thoughts, or depression. I was notified by medical staff if one requested psychotropic medication not previously prescribed. If symptoms were noted, a transfer to the Medical Center for Federal Inmates at Springfield, Missouri, was arranged. The transfer served the purpose of providing adequate psychiatric care and a bus ride. For some, the bus ride and fresh air may have been as therapeutic as the psychiatric treatment.

Each inmate was provided thirty minutes out of their cell to shower, walk, or use the available weights. To avoid the passing of contraband, a recreation area was set up away from the cells. Finding a balance between security and mental health often was challenging.

Visits by unit managers, case managers, correctional counselors, representatives from the education department, and medical personnel further reduced the isolation. The education representative was able to find most books inmates requested because several local libraries made their books available.

I spent much of my time interviewing inmates in segregation and the Control Unit. Two segregation units served different functions. Those charged with violating institutional infractions were housed in one segregation unit. The other unit housed transfers and those needing to be separated from the population. This unit had the largest turnover of inmates because inmates being transferred via the bus were often housed in this unit.

One range had four cells with metal walls three feet in front and to the sides of the cell bars. The front wall had a metal door with a 'peephole,' which allowed one to see in without having to open the door. While walking the ranges, I never observed the doors closed and usually was not occupied. I was informed litigation had changed the way these cells were utilized.

There was one other unit which had fewer cells and housed a maximum of two occupants during my tenure. It was the most secure unit in the prison. The metal door at the front of the cell had an opening through which interviews were conducted and meals served. Each cell had a door in the back wall which allowed occupants to enter his own rec area.

Men convicted of high-profile charges were housed in the unit. For several reasons, it was determined the occupant was not able to safely serve their sentence in a general population. It could be assumed, if the crime had been reported on the front page of major newspapers, the offender would be housed in a similar unit in the federal system.

Administration restricted the number of staff who had access to being on the unit. Psychologists were included on the short list and expected to visit at least monthly.

Walking the blocks of the segregation units was not a pleasant, but necessary, experience. When the front grill of a range opened for anyone other than a correctional officer, the yelling started. The yelling and profanity continued until the staff member left. The yelling included a litany of profanity I never conceptualized fitting into the same sentence.

Not all inmates were willing to talk with a psychologist. Most often, when I was informed by the individual he preferred not to be interviewed, the refusal was usually minced with words which would be considered derogatory in other settings. I honored their request and was able to gather relevant information concerning their mental health from correctional officers, unit logs, or medical staff.

After weeks and months of interviews, I became normalized visiting individuals through bars and conducting interviews in this manner. In retrospect, I wonder how one becomes comfortable talking with people in these situations. Realizing these circumstances were anything but normal led me to leave the prison system. Even now, I wonder if people 'chose' to be on segregation status in a penitentiary. I wondered what options they had as they went through a life which led to these circumstances. Was it karma, predestination, or bad genetics? I was sure no one would intentionally plan this as a life goal. How I ended up with a clipboard, tie, a set of keys, and the opportunity to go home each night was appreciated. I had to ask if the psychological visits ensured the inmates were adjusting or if I was condoning and allowing the 'system' to keep these humans acclimated to anything but a humane situation.

'Now We've Got You'

"Now we've got you!" (a bit more descriptive and graphic) two inmates said to a correctional counselor and me one spring afternoon in a segregation unit. As we turned around to see who would use such a phrase, two inmates had broken mop handles pointed at our solar plexus. Tom and I looked silently at the two on the other side of the weapons.

Although we knew a hostage situation could happen, we rationalized it would happen to someone else. It happened, and I was one of the hostages. I was sure this would never happen to me because I was one of the staff having received hostage negotiation from the FBI.

As we stood still and barely breathing, I heard the cell block door open and sound of officers rushing into the unit. While neither of us looked behind, we knew the alarm had been sounded, and correctional officers were responding to the emergency.

An officer asked the hostage takers how they got out of the recreation yard and how they got weapons. While I thought the questions were irrelevant to the situation, we were told they climbed over the twelve-foot fence with concertina wire on top, made their way into the unit unescorted without cuffs, and broke two mop handles near the outside door.

A lieutenant tried reasoning by stating the situation could be resolved if the weapons were handed to him. While a reasonable proposition, surrendering weapons was not the objective of taking hostages. Rather, they intended to use hostages to escape. During these interchanges, the counselor and I stood still, watching our hostage takers. Both of us knew the inmates, and both hostage takers had been sentenced to enough years never to be released. I understood any conviction for what was happening would not add one day to their sentences.

As the lieutenant continued encouraging them to lay down their weapons, I heard one of the officers suggest taking the fire hose out of its storage area, turning up the water pressure, and knocking the inmates down. I must still have been breathing because I remember saying we were between the fire hose and hostage takers with the plan pushing us into the weapons.

Included in the conversation between the two groups was the fact the government did not negotiate hostage situations. While the policy was intended to protect potential hostages, I did not feel protected or encouraged at the time. As the situation continued, more correctional officers entered the unit. The two with the broken mop handles must have realized there was no safe passage. They agreed to hand the weapons to me and have me escort them to their cells. I was handed the two weapons and passed them to an officer as we walked through the assembled group. All were aware of possible physical repercussions by the staff, but all also knew there would be no violence if I were in the area.

The three of us walked to their cells without a word. Once they entered their respective cells, I yelled to close both cell doors. As I walked back, I realized I had escorted two unsuccessful hostage takers without assistance or cuffs, who, minutes before, had been willing to trade my life for their freedom.

Afterward, I went into the staff bathroom and cried. The helpless feeling during the event was one I had never experienced before or since. I do not recall if the officers were still in the unit or how long I was in the bathroom. I was told to report to the Warden's office. I was still trembling when I arrived. He explained he had been taken hostage while a correctional officer at Alcatraz. The situation at Alcatraz lasted longer and was more brutal than today. Although we had heard the story, he never discussed the details. He told me to go home for the rest of the day and reminded me the best thing to do after falling off a horse was to get back on as quickly as possible. He said he wanted to see me in his office at 7:30 a.m. What the warden meant, regardless of my emotions, I was to return the next day. I agreed to return because I knew he had my best interests in mind. Like most administrators, he could be described as a 'standup guy.' (More in a later chapter.)

I do not recall walking out of the building or driving home. During the remainder of the day, I walked around aimlessly, cried, tried to read, and had a nightmare-filled sleep. I am sure I discussed the event with my wife, but I did not recall the conversation. In fact, I could not recall anything with numb being the feeling.

I walked into the Warden's office at 7:25 a.m. the next morning. He said he was glad I was back, and I should conduct business as usual and avoid being taken hostage. I assured him I would do my best to avoid future hostage situations. Even though we saw one another daily, the counselor and I never discussed the hostage situation. Everything was back to business as usual without any mention of the event.

A Near Hit

As I walked the range one morning, a resident threw a star foam cup of fermented human waste at me. Fortunately, I saw the movement from the corner of my eye and moved fast enough to miss the concoction. After throwing the cup, he started laughing and yelling he had thrown crap at the Associate Warden. The guy in the next cell told him I was not the Associate Warden but one of the psychologists. The cup thrower said, "Oh man! I apologize because I thought you were the Associate Warden."

After he apologized, I realized I had the upper hand. I smiled, back up to his cell, and began a conversation. The conversation started by me asking why he would throw human waste on anyone, why he found humor in his actions, and if he had ever been treated for a mental disorder. Answers to the first two questions were vague, but he assured me he was not a 'nut job.' I explained the type of aggression demonstrated could be considered a mental disorder, and I would regularly check regarding his adjustment. If there were similar behaviors, I would recommend a psychiatric evaluation at the hospital facility in Springfield, Missouri. I would see and chat with him regularly. No similar incidents were reported, and after a couple of weeks, he returned to the general population. From time to time, he would come by the office. Other than breaking the monotony of the day, he did not seem to want anything other than validation. Occasionally, we would laugh about the circumstances under which we met.

Welcome to the Jungle

One morning, I received a call asking me to come to one of the segregation units. When I arrived, the officer explained the inmate in the last cell was lying under the bed frame with his mattress over him. Getting him to talk through the cell bars was difficult, so I requested his cell be opened to assist him further. As I entered the cell, I saw a person so stressed he could not talk and was near a catatonic stupor. Finally, he shared he had been gang-raped the night before. He would not provide the names of the rapists and did not recall details because he eventually passed out.

When he was located, he was moved to the segregation unit for protection. A physician's assistant had already visited and dispensed medication to lower his anxiety and crying. The medication had not yet taken effect. I suggested he be moved to the hospital and placed in a strip cell to prevent suicidal attempts. Another reason to transfer was the residents in the unit knew what happened and were harassing him. The transfer to the hospital meant less time to monitor but frequent enough to assure his safety. Within days he was transferred to the medical facility where he would stay a long time.

CHAPTER 6

TALES FROM THE CONTROL UNIT

Unit Team

Each unit had a team assigned to address the business aspects of their unit. The team consisted of a unit manager, case manager, correctional counselor, educational representative, and psychologist. The unit manager was a mid-management administrator who worked with departments to ensure the unit was operating satisfactorily and with adequate security. The case manager was responsible for keeping updated records of inmates. The correctional counselor was a senior correctional officer who distributed mail and made phone calls for inmates. Both the educational representative and psychologist were 'attached' with offices in a different part of the prison but responded to requests.

While I worked on each unit, I felt most comfortable with the team in the Control unit. During the brief time, there was no chief psychologist, the unit manager, Charles, assured me not to worry because he would teach me everything I needed to know about prisons and inmates. During my internship, Charles would make a comment, turn to me, and say, 'make sure you make an entry in your notebook, Doc.' I always had a clipboard and a notepad in my pocket where I wrote the 'profound' sayings being shared.

Charles was always smoking a pipe, was able to address confrontational inmates, and had a positive comment for everyone except for the violent situations. He was the facility's most colorful staff member and could lighten crises. His experience in dealing with the staff and inmates assigned to the unit kept it quiet. At the time, an inmate in the Control Unit told me he did not have front teeth because of an altercation at USP-Atlanta, Georgia, where Charles, as a lieutenant, had physical contact with him. While relating the story, the inmate smiled, stated he was younger and had it coming. In retrospect, he reminded me of the saying, 'speak softly and carry a big stick.'

Each inmate assigned to the Control Unit had been involved in a violent situation resulting in the injury of a staff or fellow inmate. Some of the inmates and their situations included national press coverage. At times, I was interviewing some whose names had been recently taken off the most wanted list or pictured in the post office.

Referrals were reviewed and, if accepted, closely monitored. Those accepted had been involved in murder or other serious offenses while in the custody of the prison system. Several measures focused on the well-being of those housed in the unit. The unit team reviewed the progress of all assigned to the unit monthly. The Assistant Director of the Bureau of Prisons would interview each inmate in the unit on a quarterly basis. It was further mandated each inmate have a psychological interview monthly. Since the average stay on the unit was eighteen months, I was able to establish a working relationship with many. As a result of the frequency of my visits and the length of time on the unit, I was able to conduct research which became my dissertation.

James

I mentioned James in Chapter 5, where we met while he was in the general population. He was the 'concerned' parent requesting a telephone call regarding his daughter, which materialized into an escape attempt utilizing an airplane. During our frequent conversations, he asked if I thought he was insane. My answer was I knew he was dangerous but not insane. He responded some of the most prestigious psychiatrists in the Midwest testified in court he was insane and should be found Not Guilty by Reasons of Insanity on more than one occasion. The third time he was charged with putting the lives of others in danger, he was in a federal court, found guilty, and sentenced to serve time in the custody of the federal prison system.

He was the friendliest, most social person I had ever met. He was outgoing, had a great sense of humor, and could be described as charismatic. He was able to engage anyone in a conversation. When describing the event leading to his referral to the unit or events of prior criminal activity, he would openly describe the events, including the names of the deceased woman as well as others involved in his plot. He presented the information like a friend discussing a trip from one grocery store to another. There were no emotions or remorse evidenced. The way he related the story could be described as a disappointment. The disappointment came from his perception such a well-thought-out plan was unsuccessful.

A television was installed in each cell to reduce symptoms of stimulus deprivation. When placed in a setting with minimum stimulation, most individuals begin showing symptoms of cognitive difficulty. Those symptoms were discussed in the chapter on segregation units. Most inmates would have their television on regardless of whether they were watching a show or not. Cable television was not provided, but there were several local channels. One of the regular anchors on the local six o'clock news was an attractive female. James started sending her letters commenting on her hairstyle, color combinations of her wardrobe, and manner of presenting the news. Eventually, he got her attention, and she agreed to marry him after a few visits to the prison visiting room. Staff was amazed a successful, attractive woman would marry someone who had no chance of getting out of jail this century. Further, the system did not allow conjugal visits.

While in the Control Unit, James announced his candidacy for the President of the United States. Considering his self-esteem, I was not surprised but wondered how successful a campaign would be in his situation. At the time, federal inmates had unlimited access to postage stamps. This provided access to unlimited resources via the United States Postal Service. He mailed multiple letters daily to potential contributors or volunteers to work in his campaign. When the federal prison changed its policy to six stamps a month, his campaign lost momentum.

He would hold press conferences and meetings in the Control Unit for the first few months if elected. After the inconvenience placed on everyone, he would pardon himself and move to the White House. While I never took any offers I received from inmates seriously, being offered the Secretary of Education during his presidency was flattering. Knowing his history and diagnosis, I was sure the offer was not real. On the other hand, the previous offer of driving a getaway car was less attractive after I had the opportunity to work in the White House.

His platform was based on openly acknowledging being a criminal. He assured those voting for him they would know he was a crook before elected to a political office. He was not elected. In fact, I did not see his name on the ballot. After this generous, but unrealistic offer, I accepted the reality of carrying a lunch box to work daily (I hope the reader enjoys the humor I try to interject in some situations in which I found myself).

Kevin

Kevin informed me, while President Reagan had been governor of California, he had been incarcerated in a prison/ hospital for inmates with explosive disorders. During his stay, he had a frontal lobotomy to reduce the rage response. Based on the stories and events I witnessed, the surgery was ineffective. Kevin continued having episodes of rage which gave him tremendous strength. During one of his episodes, he was rumored to grab the metal toilet bolted to the back wall of a cell with an arm on each side and pull the support bolts out of the concrete wall.

One morning, he asked if we could privately talk off the range. Like most on the unit, Kevin was on a three-man order. Anytime he was taken out of his cell, he wore handcuffs and had three officers escorting him. Because Kevin could break the chain links between the standard set of cuffs by pulling his hands apart, a set of cuffs specially made for him consisted of two leg irons with a link from a tow chain connecting them.

Kevin was cuffed and taken out of his cell with three officers escorting him to the office. During our talk, he wore cuffs while the officers watched through the plexiglass window. During the meeting, he shared information about a future escape attempt. I reminded him I would have to report such information to the administration. Kevin stated he understood. His concern was the safety of inmates and staff if the plan became a reality. While it was not mentioned, I gathered he might have also been concerned about his safety.

I went to the captain's office as Kevin returned to his cell. Kevin was moved to a different part of the prison later in the day because his report was accurate, with the planned attempt thwarted. Soon after the foiled escape plan, Kevin was transferred to an undisclosed location. Kevin agreed to an interview with a weekly evening news show three years later. Those watching his interview were aware of the facility where he was housed. I was intrigued by his agreeing to the interview after the transfer, which involved several agencies working in tandem for his safety. Apparently, Kevin enjoyed appearances on national television more than concern about the safety of his life.

Two Cartons of Cigarettes

I learned the quickness of the ability to communicate with the general population from the Control Unit when it concerned my safety. Two days before the lesson concerning the 'grape vine 'of the prison, I was in the unit making my rounds. One of the guys asked if I had a book he could read. I had a book and quickly filled his request. I suggested we discuss it after he finished. The following morning, Keith came to my office to inform me a contract had been placed on my life. I listened closely to Keith's details but even more closely when he told me the name of the individual who placed the contract (Chapter 5, "The Rest of the Story"). Keith suggested I deal with the concern as quickly as possible because now he had a similar contract out for him.

Because of a history of murder, I decided to meet with Everett before leaving for the day. I went to the unit and asked if we could talk to which he agreed. I explained I knew about the contract and wanted to make things right between us. His first question was the name of the person who shared the information. After explaining I would never reveal the individual's name to anyone, we moved on.

Everett explained the contract went out because I was trying to brainwash him by asking him to read, then discuss the book. I explained my intentions were not subversive. Instead, I reminded him he asked for a book, and I handed him the one I had. Based on the title, 'I'm OK, You're OK,' he assumed I was attempting to alter and control his thinking.

Everett was of the impression I was from the education department, which provided reading material. After I explained I was a psychologist, he realized the source of the confusion, returned the book, and asked me to forward his request to the education department.

After we resolved the situation, he asked if I would pull him off the range to talk. Despite his history and the recent contract, the request was honored. Each time we met, he was cuffed, the cell door opened, he was scanned for contraband, and three correctional officers escorted him. While the officers observed through the Plexiglas window, we discussed his early childhood, his life experiences, military service, and the two escape attempts resulting in the death of at least one correctional officer during each attempt. Prior to his arrival, he had killed three individuals. It was no surprise he was in the supermax unit of the prison system. There were several precautions taken when moving him out of his cell. However, sharpened instruments, such as toothbrushes, combs, or kitchenware made from plastic could not be detected by the scanner. In retrospect, I was fortunate Everett did not have a weapon during our meetings.

The following morning, Keith came to the office to congratulate me. He heard the contract had been cancelled and wanted to know how the conversation went with Everett. I explained we discussed his concerns and were able to work things out. Of course, I was relieved but still indignant remembering another psychologist's life was worth three cartons of cigarettes and I was only worth two. It was likely Keith's intervention saved my life.

Everett and another inmate bludgeoned two officers on the unit several months later. One officer was a fair and respected man with six months before his retirement. He had plans to spend time with his grandchildren. The death was reported to let rival gangs know anyone could be killed at any time. I was already at my next assignment in Virginia and was saddened because I knew the officers. They were solid, loyal employees who were fair in their interactions with all.

Thoughts

I did not recall experiencing fear during these situations. The communications with both Keith and Everett were conducted in a business-like fashion with neither showing emotions. I knew the danger when dealing with them as well as the fact taking the life of another person was not novel to either. I recall looking down at my trouser legs during the conversation with Everett and noticed the legs of my trousers was shaking. From the shaking trousers, I gathered my legs were shaking and I was anxious. However, during the conversation I did not consciously experience emotions. While the topic was him placing a contract on my life, one watching the conversation would have thought we were discussing another losing season for the Chicago Cubs or local news.

I cannot explain, nor understand, why I felt no fear during these and similar situations. The only time I recall feeling fear was after being taken hostage. At other times, I felt no fear nor questioned involving myself in dangerous situations. The explanation may include my military training. As an Infantry officer, I was trained to be aware of danger but to remain rational for the safety of my troops.

KENNETH KOHUTEK, PH.D.

Another factor which contributed to my calm was the awareness of the number of correctional staff who could be counted on. Regardless of where I was or what I was doing, I knew someone always had my back. As a result, I responded to each alarm which I hoped was comforting to my fellow staff members. On one occasion, I noticed I was the only non-correctional staff at the emergency. It was my impression any emergency needed all available to assist. My friends had a different explanation: they thought I was suicidal but unwilling to take my own life. Therefore, placing myself in harm's way was not an issue. They may have been correct. My take included the fact I was doing my job to the best of my ability. It was my intention to reduce the violence during volatile situations. All involved knew I was fair and handled each situation in a professional manner.

CHAPTER 7

———◦◦◦◦———

THE CLINIC/HOSPITAL

Clinical Staff

Each of the clinical staff were professional, cordial, and easy to work with. The staff consisted of the hospital administrator, an assistant administrator, two physicians, a dentist, and 10 Physician Assistants. Consultants, including a psychiatrist, would visit every two weeks. PA coverage was available 24 hours a day and every day of the year.

Toward the end of my time at Marion, I moved my office to the clinic. I thought the climate in prison was becoming more volatile, and I felt more comfortable with the additional staff in the clinic. The hospital administrator approved the request to move my office. I asked the orderly to find one of his friends, and the move took place. I had never seen two men pick up an executive-size desk and move it without difficulty. Working out in the weight shack paid off! Watching the move had to remind staff of the strength of those who spent time in the weight shack, and potential difficulty should a full-scale riot occur.

Relocating an office required the approval of several departments, which might take months. My theory was, if one moved with authority and walked quickly, no one would question the action. All involved would assume an upline administrator had already approved the request. In this case, begging forgiveness was better than asking permission. There was no doubt concern about the security of this penitentiary would be tantamount with few concerned about a psychologist moving his office. Because of drugs available in the clinic, it was common knowledge the hospital would be the first place to be taken over if a riot should occur. Nevertheless, I felt safer there than in a long corridor with only two offices in use. Moving my office meant the split within the department was physical as well as professional. At the time, I had no concern for the chief because I knew he only left his office to attend meetings or conferences. I did not recall ever seeing an inmate in his office during the time we worked together.

One of the PA's, Pete, considered himself a Texan because his father worked at a federal prison in Texas. Since this was the first time I lived outside of Texas, we bonded. We did not have much in common, but it was good to have a friend. He was single, while I was married with a child. He smoked cigarettes and marijuana, but I smoked neither. He drank a lot of beer, while I was a social drinker. He had a black belt in Taekwondo, while the only belt I had was black, but it was used to hold up my slacks. He kept a boa constrictor in his apartment, and I tried to avoid the reptile. Nevertheless, I stayed at his apartment when I served as Duty Officer.

Each time I was called to a unit, I assumed it a crisis which involved mental health issues. As soon as I got the call, I asked Pete to be contacted if on the day shift. We would meet in the unit and were prepared to meet all situations. At times, his presence was as a backup, while at other times, he was a major player.

One afternoon I was summoned to a segregation unit because an inmate did not want to move to another cell. He needed to be moved to place another inmate where he was located. I worked with him while in the population and staff thought I could convince him without difficulty or a confrontation.

Even though we knew one another, I started the conversation by introducing myself and saying why I wanted to talk with him. I explained he needed to be moved to a quieter range as well as mentioned the cell was needed for another. I used the same words as the officers, but this time, he agreed to cooperate. Neither Pete nor I had a pair of cuffs, but the request to open his cell door was given. As his cell door opened, he pulled a set of homemade nun chucks from under his mattress. I was sure he knew how to use them the way he grabbed them. Before I could respond, Pete leaped to my left side, used a foot to push off on the metal bed frame, was in front me and took the weapon in what seemed like a nanosecond. The nun chucks were homemade, with a thin part from a sheet connecting the two pieces. Each piece consisted of a part of the sheet in the center to connect both sides, newspaper wrapped tightly around the pieces of sheets, with each side held together with tape.

The situation was neutralized, and the transfer was made without complications. All staff believed he did not want to move because the weapon would be discovered. Information regarding the weapon was reported to the captain's office, and the situation was dealt with according to institutional guidelines. Once again, violence had been avoided.

Cecil

The advantage of moving my office to the clinic proved useful because several confined worked with both the clinic and psychology. An example was Cecil, a six-foot, six-inch-tall man who filled his tall frame and had tremendous strength. His upper left arm was disfigured because he had been hit with shotgun pellets during an attempted bank robbery. Cecil had been diagnosed with a schizophrenic disorder but could function while on his medication.

The officer on the unit contacted the captain's office regarding Cecil's erratic behavior. Those in the office knew I had been working with him for almost a year and contacted me, stating Cecil was yelling in the cell block. To complicate the issue, the yelling involved Cecil stated he wanted to sexually be with another who would be described as a 'female.' Issues of concern included he had discontinued taking his medication and the person with whom he was enamored had a partner.

The gold standard was to isolate the situation as quickly and quietly as possible. Based on Cecil's deteriorated mental status, but still being communicative, he agreed to walk to the clinic unescorted. Because of his size, it seemed safer for him to come on his own volition rather than with escorts. Officers were placed along the corridor to ensure he made his way without detours or distractions.

Soon, Cecil was knocking on the clinic's metal door. I greeted and invited him to my office. He was cordial, communitive, and frequently referred to me as 'Doc.' Once we were seated, I asked him to share his perspective concerning the events in the unit. He described the infatuation with the other inmate. His speech indicated his thought process was single-mindedly focused on the one topic.

After asking and listening to his perspective, I expressed concern about his safety as well as his decision to discontinue medication without approval from the physician. Included in my concerns was his need to be reminded the individual being discussed was in a long-term relationship, his partner was in a gang, and issues related to race was a major part of their dogma.

I explained my concern three times with his response being

the same; he wanted to return to the unit to pursue his amorous attachment. My requests became more directive with each explanation until I clearly stated returning to the unit was not an option and the only choice was to be admitted to the hospital. Once again, he expressed his desire to not be in the hospital but this time raising his voice in protest. His protest was verbal, with no posturing or physical threats. I trusted his contact with reality was sufficient to know I meant no harm. Knowing there was backup available was another reason to continue our conversation.

On the fourth exchange, I informed him the desire to return to the unit was not an option. As he protested, I continued explaining the plan. I informed him several officers had made their way to the clinic and were standing outside the door.

In response to his doubting my information, I encouraged him to see for himself. When opening the door, Cecil found himself staring eye to eye with a lieutenant who was larger than himself. Behind the lieutenant were eight officers. Cecil was surprised, smiled sheepishly while greeting the lieutenant, and shut the door.

I explained we would be going to the hospital ward, and, this time, he reluctantly acquiesced. Once he and I were in the elevator, the elevator was filled with as many officers as could fit into the small space (I was sure we exceeded the recommended weight restriction). The elevator was so full, none of us were able to raise our hands and all kept their hands to their side.

After the elevator reached the hospital, Cecil and I walked to the ward with a previously full elevator of officers in tow. Once on the ward, Cecil stated he had changed his mind and did not want to be in the hospital or restart his medication. Instead, he stated he wanted to return to his unit. Cecil was encouraged to take the few steps needed to be in a room. Before I could respond, he grabbed my right arm with his injured left arm, and I was moved across the tile without having moved my feet. The lieutenant sternly told Cecil to let go of my arm and enter the room. I felt like I was standing between the twin towers during those moments. They stared at one another, and eventually, Cecil let go of my arm and entered the room.

It was encouraging to know Cecil responded to our requests without physical force. He was quickly transferred to the medical facility, restarted his medication, and returned with symptoms in remission. He stopped by my office at least once a week. During those meetings, neither of us mentioned his previous love triangle. Instead, the discussion focused on his adjustment and the need to continue his medication.

A Fifteen-Minute Watch

The associate warden called me into his office one morning and explained my responsibility was to observe a prisoner on the hospital ward until I was told otherwise. The person I was to observe was on suicide watch and to be checked at least every fifteen minutes. I asked if there was additional information. He explained the person was a state inmate, was to be kept alive, and I was assigned to prevent him from taking his life. During his stay in the federal prison system, it was tantamount to prevent him from self-harm or suicide. The person I was assigned to watch had been sentenced to be executed the following week and we were expected to keep him alive until the state retook custody.

The person I watched was in a stripped hospital room with a blanket, mattress, and underwear. We talked from time to time, but he preferred being alone. On the fifth day, I went to the ward, and he was gone. I was told the state came to place him in their custody because his execution was to be the next day. Working to try to keep a person alive so he could be executed was another interesting responsibility.

CHAPTER 8

THE CAMP

The minimum-security camp attached to the facility had no fences or towers. Usually, one correctional officer and unit team were on duty during the day. Fraud or embezzlement was the most common conviction, while others were approaching the end of their sentence and transferred to the camp to assist in acclimating to life without living in a cell. Often, a person of national notoriety was sent to serve their sentence. All were considered low escape risks. I do not recall hearing about someone 'escaping' from a camp. It would not be much of an escape because it would be walking away.

Events leading to a conviction were often unusual. One involved the result of a strong storm which destroyed rice crops in the south. Prior to planting, farmers had the option to insure their crops in the event of a disaster, such as the storm. The company which provided this opportunity was backed by the federal government.

The process of applying for crop loss, included the submission of pictures, documenting the damage. Two neighboring farmers, both of whom suffered crop damage, decided to pool their pictures. After reviewing the collection, each sent in those which showed the worse damage. Unfortunately, the individual to whom the pictures were sent recognized the ruse and the farmers were sentenced to serve federal time. They were embarrassed and more concerned about what their family's and church members would think than what might happen to them during their incarceration. Both were sure their reputations would be ruined in the small rural community they called home. They could not relocate because their livelihood came from the fields they farmed. Both complied with every rule and guideline while at the camp. While their sentences were short, I do not think they were released in time for the next spring planting.

Another situation started in the back of a family-owned print shop and several bottles of whiskey. The shop owner and a friend were unwinding from the week and decided to print counterfeit money while in their inebriated condition. They selected the paper and ink they thought would pass as US currency from their inventory. After making the model of a twenty-dollar bill, they printed off several thousand dollars of their newly found riches. It was agreed the best way to spend their money was to travel to the Ozarks and make purchases in isolated stores. They were enthusiastic when they purchased a pack of cigarettes and got change. Within a few minutes, a state trooper pulled them over, confiscated their fortune, and arrested them for trying to pass counterfeit money. It seemed the store owner, who happened to be a retired FBI agent, contacted the authorities immediately. The same day I talked with these gentlemen, I knew the best counterfeiter known to the Treasury Department was housed in the nearby penitentiary. The artist was not necessarily dangerous, but the Treasury Department was concerned about his receiving help from the outside to assist in his escape. There are limited funds in any bank robbery. There was no idea how many of his twenty-dollar bills were in circulation.

Besides interviewing individuals who were new to the system,

I would visit the camp once a week. One evening while heading to my vehicle, I noticed a low-flying Cessna which appeared out of control on a course headed toward the prison. Within one hundred yards from the concertina fences, the plane landed. The next morning, I learned a female from Chicago had commissioned a pilot and his plane to fly over southern Illinois to view real estate. As the plane went south, the passenger pulled out a revolver and instructed the pilot to follow her instructions. The plane's course was changed, and when the pilot saw the towers, he realized what was about to happen.

While flying the plane, the pilot wrestled the weapon from her, fired a round, and landed in the cleared perimeter surrounding the prison. She commissioned the wrong pilot because he spent several years flying various aircraft in Vietnam. The officers in the towers watching the incident reported two inmates were standing in the middle of an 'X' made of torn bedsheets.

I felt a sense of relieve when it was determined the two standing on the 'X' were the same two who requested a phone call to coordinate a visit from a social worker and his daughter. Fortunately, the individual did not answer her phone.

Thanks to an alert and well-trained pilot, the escape attempt was foiled.

CHAPTER 9

MEANWHILE, BACK IN THE PSYCHOLOGY DEPARTMENT

A New Chief

As you may recall, the two psychologists at the penitentiary when I started my internship transferred to other facilities after the therapeutic community closed. Fortunately, a consultant psychologist from the local university would come in one afternoon a week to assist, provide feedback, and listen to my concerns. The regional psychologist was always available and promptly called back if he missed my call. After three weeks, I received a call from an individual who introduced himself, stating he was the new chief psychologist and would be on board in two weeks.

To say the new chief was a buffoon would be an insult to the buffoons of the world! It was as if the administrators in the Central Office looked for the ineptest person in the prison system, gave him a promotion/ raise, and sent him here. Many expressed concern his previous assignment was at a minimum-security coeducational facility. The atmosphere from which he was coming was a world apart, less volatile, and dangerous than where he would be in two weeks. I do not think, once he arrived at this facility, he ever realized his need to be an authority figure and talk down to staff and inmates created more difficulty than assistance. But who was I to question the decision of the Bureau of Prisons under the Department of Justice? I was halfway through my internship year without the Ph.D. behind my name and still a student.

Where Did He Come From?

At some point in the past, the federal government operated two substance abuse programs. The programs were closed, and infrastructure transferred to the Bureau of Prisons. It was agreed the staff of the treatment centers would be provided the opportunity to continue working at the physical location. The fact a rehab program was staffed with personnel in the rehabilitation departments with few, if any correctional officers, created a dilemma while placing some staff members. Consequently, the staff compliment was organized to meet the needs of a prison which resulted in some staff transferred to other responsibilities.

One staff member from this group had a doctorate in education and reassigned to the psychology department. The training for the Ed.D. is not better or worse than a Ph.D., but the curriculum is different and prepares the graduate for different responsibilities. Both had a doctor in their title, so they could easily be interchanged, right? Not so much!

It was obvious from the first day his training was not in psychology. His background was common knowledge because he discussed his training and degrees with all who would listen. During the three or four years we worked together, I can safely say he had no idea what he was supposed to be doing. The administration acknowledged concerns and asked me to pick up the slack.

The administration decided he would be a better fit in the role of serving on committees rather than working behind the grills. While the chief psychologist, as a department head, had the responsibility of being on committees, his role was expanded to include serving on all committees, as well as represent the facility at meeting/conferences sponsored by outside agencies. All agreed the decision helped the prison flow more smoothly. His confrontational manner and arrogance made every contact with an inmate an opportunity to incite violence. Dealing with those serving one, two or more life sentences did not work. More than once, I heard the phrase, "What are they going to do? Give me another life sentence?"

Due to the division of labor, my responsibilities were to tend to the clinical needs of the general population and segregation units. While walking the segregation units was not my favorite assignment, the work was interesting because people had different stories. My responsibilities included identifying those experiencing psychiatric issues either prior to, or because of being on segregation status. Those in need of additional assistance were referred to the consultant psychiatrist.

Besides my work on the segregation units, more from the general population requested to be seen. I attributed the increase to being visible in the units, walking the ranges (which few other than the correctional staff did), and walking the corridors. Many requests were to have a place to chat with a person who went home every night while others had issues which needed to be addressed. Those stopping by to chat were scheduled on a biweekly or three-week schedule. The others were seen more often. My schedule was to have sessions in my office during mornings, while I spent afternoons in segregation units.

When I was having a session, or when the orderly for the corridor was present, the metal door at the end of the psychology corridor was locked. I was aware of this vulnerability and asked an officer to check the corridor from time to time. The officer walking through the corridor may not have prevented me from harm but provided the sense of security needed to perform my job.

An Added Responsibility

At the end of workdays, I became accustomed to waking my boss before leaving. One afternoon, I saw boots propped on the desk, the chief kicked back in his chair, and taking a nap. I chose not to wake him. The following morning every correctional officer I saw on my way to the office informed me the captain wanted to see me as soon as possible. I had learned when the captain wanted to talk with me was not good and worse when all correctional staff knew about the meeting. Our conversations usually involved an incident where someone I followed had issues due to a psychiatric diagnosis, there was an upcoming event which may result in mental health issues or assist an officer in writing an Incident Report.

I made my way to the Captain's office where he was holding a meeting. He interrupted his meeting and asked me to come in. In front of the lieutenants, he expressed concern and reminded me all keys and key rings had to be accounted for at the end of each shift. If a key, or key ring, was missing, the person who checked out the keys would be called and required to return to the facility to return the keys. I reminded him I had worked here for several years and was aware of the policy. He assured me he knew I was aware of the policy, but I needed to be reminded. He wanted me to know several officers used valuable time searching for a missing set of keys the previous afternoon. My chief had not turned in the keys issued him. A lieutenant called his residence and discovered he had not gotten home. The obvious conclusion was he would be on campus. Missing keys were an indicator a person would still be on campus and may have been dumped somewhere. An officer found him with his feet still propped on his desk and sleeping.

The captain, tongue in cheek, reminded me my job description included a phrase stating, 'and other responsibilities as assigned.' He told me one of my added responsibilities was to wake my supervisor before I left for the day. Waking him was critical so there would not have to be concern he had been stuck in a dumpster. We all laughed at this assignment, and I set out for another day of adventure. I would daily check to ensure his feet were on the floor until I transferred.

Moving Forward

At some point, my internship ended without ceremony. I surmised I had performed satisfactorily during the year because I was offered the opportunity to continue working at Marion. Since I had not completed my degree, I was assigned to the Research Department. Responsibilities of this position included completing reports requested by various agencies in the Justice Department, completing reports requested by administrators at the facility, and completing my dissertation. My days of research were before computers could crunch massive amounts of data in seconds. I gathered data, analyzed, and authored reports with my pencil and a handheld calculator.

Responsibilities of the research department included the organization of a committee to review proposals, provide feedback to the individual who presented the proposal, as well as working with the research department at the Central Office with proposals approved by our institutional committee. Most of the requests were denied because of confidentiality or offering incentives which violated guidelines. One of the proposals was approved and referred to the research department at the Central Office. The rigor of the reviews on the Central Office was even greater, with most proposals being denied. The denials frustrated university faculty who had applied for tenure and needed to publish. The guidelines for research with incarcerated individuals were strict and intended to protect those whose consent to participate may be the result of perceived coercion or believe there may be more benefits than allowed by institutional guidelines.

Being a member of the research department, I had the opportunity to author several reports related to the prison and the long-term segregation unit, also known as the Control or H unit. I drafted more research papers than anyone before or since.

A project the Regional Research Administrator and I completed was the development of a regression equation designed to predict those who might be escape risks. I collected data from both USP-Marion and USP-Atlanta, Georgia. After weeks of analyzing the data, an equation which accounted for 90% of attempted or actual escapes was developed. Tom, the regional administrator, was ecstatic. He reminded me the equation must be tried on the general population to assess its validity. After more days of collecting and analyzing data, the equation was shredded. Comparing the predictive validity with the general population indicated ALL the population fit the criteria of being an escape risk. We learned from the exercise we were either not considering the correct variables or most incarcerated at this facility were escape risks. In retrospect, most of those housed in this facility would be considered escape risks. It would have been interesting to utilize this equation in less secure facilities.

The realities of working in a penitentiary prevented additional work. Another riot occurred with those in the education, psychology, and research departments assigned to the kitchen to make hundreds of sandwiches. By the time things returned to 'normal,' other priorities took precedence.

Even though I was assigned to the research department, and under the supervision of the Regional Research Administrator, I spent a portion of my time in the psychology department to assist in the department requirements. The fact I remained in the same office made it easy for others to assume I had the same responsibilities. I continued meeting with the 'regulars' as well as interviews on the segregation units.

In between assignments, I found time to work on my dissertation. The process started with designing a study to meet the approval of both the prison and dissertation committees. It was not an easy task, but the biggest challenges were in front of me. After developing a plan, I wrote the two proposals, one which would be reviewed by the bureau's research committee, with the other reviewed by the dissertation advisor on my university campus. I was aware one would be bogged down in bureaucracy, while the other required attention from the dissertation advisor who was six hundred-eighty miles and ten hours away. My submitted revisions would sit on his desk for months before I received a reply. The saying 'the squeaky wheel gets greased' proved to be true. To expedite the process, I used vacation time to meet monthly with the advisor. In retrospect, he was the most qualified to chair the dissertation committee but either a procrastinator or overwhelmed with work. Neither was my concern because my goal was to complete the research and degree.

After months of anticipation, I was ecstatic when both committees approved the proposal! Next came the challenging steps; I needed to recruit volunteers from both the Control Unit and general population to participate in the study. It was necessary to seek willing participants, explain the purpose of the study, as well as a provide a clear explanation of any benefits there might be because of completing the study. Obtaining a signature was a challenge because most by participating were guarded and did not trust most people on staff.

After the hurdle of getting signed Consent Forms from enough participants to have a reasonable sample size, all left to do was collect pre-treatment data, conduct the study, collect post-treatment data, write the results, and present my findings to the dissertation committee. During the final defense of my work, I fielded questions from the relevant to mundane. At the end of the inquisition, I had the opportunity to listen to how I had been transformed from a dunce when arriving on campus to becoming one worthy of having the Ph.D. attached to my name. Another example of making a 'silk purse out of a sow's ear'!

A unique characteristic about the paper was it was the sample because it was the first and, the only study successfully completed on the Control Unit. The fact I understood the limitations of a study in prison and wrote the proposal to align with the requirements helped earn the approval of the central office. Another factor contributing to this project's success was the familiarity participants had with me. A peer-reviewed professional journal published the study.

With the dissertation, including the final defense, I graduated having earned the Ph.D. I requested and was transferred into a full-time psychology position. While I enjoyed my days in research, I thought I would have a better chance of making a difference in psychology and knew I would move up the GS rankings faster.

Back to the Psychology Department

Even though I had never left the psychology department, I was now formally a staff psychologist. I had the same responsibilities as an intern and while overseeing the research. The primary difference was movement up the GS rating and an increase in my salary. I did not need an orientation to the facility, tours, or any greeting because most with whom I worked did not notice the changes in my different titles. The pay raise was nice, but to formally be a 'real' psychologist and finally earned the title 'Doc' was rewarding. After years of investing time, tuition, as well as dealing with usual stressful events was a relief to put those years behind me.

During the years in the doctoral program, at one time or another, I was a part-time loader with UPS, a full-time manager of a small clothing store, worked at a service station, tutored statistics, held several parttime positions in the psychology department, was a full-time staff member at the local mental health department and, finally, a part-time research assistant at the Federal Correctional Institute in Seagoville, Texas. Because I was on an academic delay from the Army, I was required to be a full-time student each semester. A person from my Control Group reviewed my schedule and grades annually. A document from the graduate school was requested each year documenting I was making satisfactorily progress toward the completion of my degree. As a graduate student during the 1970's, I sported a full beard and ponytail common in those years. Eventually, I traded my low quarter shoes for sandals.

I was ordered to report once a year for a physical. The annual physical meant a shave and short hair prior to reporting. I did not receive a stipend or salary from the Army during those years. My original branch was Field Artillery but was later assigned to

Medical Services. At my request, I had another branch transfer before reporting to active duty to Infantry and received a DD214 after completion of my commitment.

Finally, the dissertation was completed, the defense was successful, and I graduated having earned the Ph.D. I requested and was transferred into a full-time psychology position. While I enjoyed my days in research, I thought I might have a better chance of making a difference in the system as a psychologist and knew I would move up the GS ratings faster.

After leaving academia, I was able to focus on my role as a psychologist. There was the same complement of staff and I continued to report to the Chief of Psychology. Although the chief was directly over my position on the organizational chart, I would be given assignments by various administrators. Even though I did not seek assignments, it created an awkward situation in the department. When I was working on a project by an associate warden, my chief would ask what I was doing and why I would be working on the assignment. I explained I had been given the assignment by his boss to which he would clear his throat and say, "I guess you need to finish it." While never discussed, there was tension between us because of those assignments. Once he asked why I was given the assignment to which I answered I was not sure, and he needed to check with the associate warden to learn the answer.

Interestingly, the chief had not changed his approach to dealing with the staff or inmates over the years. In fact, he became more authoritarian, which may or may not may have been the result of his perceived competition in the department. The complaints from line staff and inmates contributed to the discord in the department. He would attempt to gloss over the issue, but daily the conflict was obvious and noticeable to others. I would stay away from my office for a week at a time to avoid the chill. Eventually, the move to the clinic was the 'straw breaking the camel's back' and communication between us stopped.

I was told the embellishment regarding his past accomplishments had increased and, more than once, was told he had not given an accurate description of his life. Embellishment was a polite word because many of his stories were outright lies. At times, his stories would come under question by others in meetings. A staff member who attended the same meetings told the chief he had to be four hundred years old to have accomplished what he claimed. One example of his life stories occurred during World War II. During those years, he had been in a Japanese concentration camp for much of the war, as well as having been a paratrooper who experienced the most parachute jumps in the Africa and European theatre. When the accuracy was questioned, he would stutter and offer an explanation but did not answer the question. Most of the staff did not believe anything he said, so he was ignored and allowed to spin his tales unquestioned and, usually, no one listened.

Above my Pay Grade

I was given assignments over my pay grade providing me experience beyond the psychology department. An example of the assignments included being added to the Duty Officer roster, attended training classes above my level of responsibility, and attended the Warden's meetings when the chief was absent. The opportunity to play tennis and family trips to canoeing down the James River with both associate wardens would have been enough for a recommendation endorsing me to most psychology positions in the system. There were other opportunities afforded me for which I remain eternally grateful. Unfortunately, life got in the way of this career.

Duty Officer

I had the honor of being one of the youngest and only staff psychologist to be assigned the responsibility of Duty Officer. The Duty Officer was responsible for assuring the facility was safe, overseeing the operation during the weekend, and when administrative staff was not present. The Duty Officer was always on call and required to be near the prison. Since my residence was over fifty miles away, my friend Pete, the Physician's Assistant, who lived eight miles from work, agreed to let me stay at his home.

One Sunday morning, the lieutenant on duty and I were notified an assault was occurring in the law library. As Duty Officer, it was my responsibility to oversee the incident. We found two inmates assaulting a third with shanks. The three were locked in a caged area with no staff with them. During the incident, the lieutenant on duty, Jim, stood beside me and asked how to proceed. Jim had been with the system longer and had moved up to his position while starting as a correctional officer. An analogy from the military would be a seasoned sergeant asking a brand-new second lieutenant how to proceed. While the question followed protocol, it would have been foolish not to consider his recommendation. I asked what was written in the Post Orders concerning similar incidents; he told me what I already knew. When possible, we were not to put staff in harm's way. My response was to follow the Post Orders.

Eventually, the assailants stopped stabbing the victim. I assumed it was because they were sure he was dead. The two walked to the cage door, slid their weapons under the door, put their hands in the area for cuffing, and appeared prepared to be escorted to segregation. Somehow, the victim was still alive and taken to the local hospital. He recovered from his injuries and was transferred to another facility.

It was later learned all three were state inmates, with the two assaulters housed in a federal facility because of overcrowding. They arrived at separate times, and we had not been made aware of the fact the victim was to be separated from others because he had provided information to the state authorities which resulted in the thwarting of illegal behavior of other felons -- a snitch. Once the two learned why the third was at the facility, the law of the jungle went into effect. Snitches had to be removed from the population.

Warden's Meetings

Every Tuesday morning, the Warden and department heads would gather for the Warden's meeting. The purpose of the meetings was to keep all in a supervisory position informed, discuss concerns which involved more than one department, as well as describe upcoming changes. I saw it as an honor to be allowed to attend these meetings. All in the meetings treated me with respect and recognized my commitment.

I was thankful for the opportunity to attend those meetings. As a result, I gained an understanding of the bigger picture of the system. Also, my credibility was enhanced which assisted in performing my psychology duties. Staff followed my recommendations more often because they viewed me as a team player.

One cold Illinois winter Tuesday morning, there was a strong northern wind, ice was under the snow, and walking outside or driving was dangerous. The leaves had long since fallen from the trees making the landscape resemble a frozen tundra. I could attest to the danger because my drive to work was more like sliding up the highway. I was in the Tuesday Warden's meeting in warmer quarters and comfortable after a harrowing, sliding two-hour drive of the fifty miles to work.

During the meeting, the Wardens mentioned he noticed black lines between tiles he had not previously seen. Since we were on lockdown status, inmates from the camp were coming in during the night to complete orderly tasks. It was the Warden's opinion the 'campers' needed to do a better job mopping the floor before buffing. It was his impression the orderlies were either not picking up the dirt or they needed to change the mop water more often. With the floor not being correctly cleaned, buffing would result in dirt being buffed into gaps between the tiles. The captain and camp administrator both disagreed by stating the camp officer carefully selected the orderlies as well as closely supervised while completing their work.

Several department heads had their own take on the dark spaces between the tiles. Being a psychologist, I had nothing to offer. While the discussion related to the warden's question continued, I counted the number of department heads, their estimated GS levels, and the approximate dollars spent on this discussion regarding the dark spaces. While doing the mental mathematics, I randomly made eye contact with the hospital administrator. Based on his facial expression, it was obvious he was having similar thoughts. The quick glance resulted in me losing control and laughing. Finally, the question was answered with the notion, during chilly weather the tiles shrunk and expanded during the summer months. The meeting ended, and we headed to our responsibilities.

Thirty minutes later, the Associate Warden of Programs came to my office. Both the warden and he were concerned about me usually being a one-person department and responsible for tending to all the facility's mental health issues. The Warden and AP agreed my time would be better spent attending to the psychological responsibilities rather than attending the weekly meetings. I was sure the AW made his way to my office because of my laughter regarding the black lines. While he was leaving the office, he turned around and, with a smile, asked if I had other ideas which would result in attending fewer meeting, I should let him know. Oh well, I learned more about tile than I had known or wanted to know.

CHAPTER 10

THOSE CHOOSING TO WORK IN A PENITENTIARY

Life after Hours

I did not attend many social functions because of the distance between home and the facility. My wife and I attended the Christmas party during my first year. It took place at an associate warden's house on campus. The associate warden's wife greeted us at the door. Smiling and with a bubbly voice, she explained the men were in the basement and, looking at my wife, said, 'Us girls are in the living room.' The administration invited all staff, but no correctional officers were in attendance. In the basement, I found the administrative staff and a couple of lieutenants drinking and listening to a record called 'Your First Day at Camp Lejeune.' The record, along with alcohol, got the adrenaline flowing in at least nine marines. It was enjoyable watching these overweight, over 40-year-olds, trying to do pushups.

My wife, who struggled with the traditional male/female stereotypes, stayed upstairs for a respectful time. However, eventually, she broke protocol and made her way to the basement and joined the men. Either she broke the barrier, or her action did not sit well with the other wives because, eventually, five or six of them found their way to the basement. I want to think, since she and I were the youngest at the function, the other wives may have been concerned about their husband's actions around this much younger woman. There may have been other explanations, but I prefer to think the other wives were jealous.

The split between correctional staff, administrators, and wives closely followed the protocol found in the military. In this setting, however, those guidelines were not spoken, but a well-entrenched part of the culture.

The Administrators

Because of the institution's mission, the warden, associate wardens, and captain had years of experience. One had been a correctional officer at USP- Alcatraz and taken hostage during one of the uprisings. He did not discuss those years with me, but it was common knowledge throughout the staff. He was a genuine, committed person who was willing to make tough decisions. While there could be criticism about his being a stickler for rules, including the beard incident, he was fair in his decisions. He would follow up with us whenever his decisions adversely impacted our lives. While always in character, he was approachable and even spent time with a fledgling intern. Loyalty was an important word to him. It was essential to know others would be standing by his side during a crisis.

While I was at the prison, the two associate wardens remained the same. Both were of the same cut as the warden. They knew their business and were approachable. Both considered themselves accomplished tennis players.

During an afternoon after losing every match and set to one of the associate wardens, I commented my game would improve if I had a racket as nice as his. He suggested I get the feel of what his racket felt like before investing in another. We traded rackets, and he continued beating me. Because of the one-sided games, we decided to play doubles. The AW's wife was as fierce as her husband, so she and I matched up against the two AWs. I got closer, but I was still on the losing side of the net. In any case, it was relaxing to play and laugh with those honorable, resolute individuals. I am sure one later retired while the other was promoted to warden.

I never heard the staff question the decisions of these administrators. They had a serious responsibility and managed it well.

The Correctional Staff

Most lieutenants were halfway through their careers with opportunities for advancement. Marion was a place to gain experience for rapid promotions. After a few years, opportunities were presented the officers would never be experienced in a less secure prison. This level of supervisors was totally business with an understanding of the seriousness of their responsibilities.

One could not have a prison without correctional officers, and this prison had plenty because it remained open twenty-four hours a day, seven days a week, three hundred and sixty-five days a year. All our correctional officers were males who ranged in age, size, and race. The local university had a master's program in Criminal Justice, and the younger officers had at least a bachelor's degree, while several had completed their master's. Most of the older guards had completed high school with a military background.

Temperaments varied between the two groups. While neither I nor anyone else administered vocational tests, I gathered the more successful correctional officers would be in the Realistic/

Conventical area of Holland's Theory of Vocations. The older guards walked slower and generally did not talk as much. In general, these officers had a sense of humor, and while away from their jobs, they would laugh but only amongst themselves.

Another unique characteristic was, regardless of how long one worked for the Bureau, once an individual resigned, the interactions ceased. I saw and experienced the reaction myself. After resigning from the prisons, I attempted to contact nine staff members with whom I had worked. Each time my former coworkers did not return my calls. I attended a conference in a city where two of my fellow psychologists worked. I contacted them asking about lunch. The one who responded seemed uncomfortable talking and spent less than thirty minutes chatting.

While the captain was responsible for the prison's security, the lieutenants supervised the daily operation. The rotation of shifts meant each worked the day shift from time to time. I believe one of the lieutenants played games with me because, when he was on the day shift, he would tell me to do something related to the correctional staff. Each time this occurred, I reminded him there was no line from his name to mine on the organizational chart. He would smile and we went our separate ways.

After lunch on my last day, he came to my office and asked if I was ready to leave. I told him my boxes were in the car. He explained they were one officer short for the afternoon, and he was assigning me to a tower. I looked at him, and we both smiled because we had similar interactions for at least two years. Then his smile grew and said he made the assignment to assure nothing happened to me during my last half day. I smiled, thanked him, and headed to my last assignment at Marion. I had been in a tower before, and familiar with their organization. He assigned me to the tower which was the least likely to have an emergency.

What I liked about the assignment was the constant chatter on the tower-to-tower radio. They included me and, amongst other things, assured me I would miss this place. My shift ended; I attended a nice going away party and drove out of the property for the last time.

There was a liquor store a mile from the prison property which could have gained a profit if opened thirty minutes a day, ten minutes after the end of each shift. One could easily recognize the prison uniforms in the parking lot and know more officers were in the parking lot than those who attended a union meeting.

The Carpool

Considering the mostly rural area around the prison, many of us traveled eighty miles a day to get to work. I learned of a carpool leaving Anna, Illinois, and asked an officer if I could join the group. The officer welcomed me and told where to meet at 7:00 am. The carpool met halfway between my home and work. With the shift changes and rotating days off, the members and the number of riders varied each morning. At times, two vehicles would journey north on Interstate 59 to work. While the group participants varied, the atmosphere stayed the same, with laughter and foolishness. The opportunity to get extra minutes of sleep was not possible with the noise. While riding in one officer's vehicle, we had the opportunity (?) to listen to motivational tapes. As a passenger, he would write in a notebook. He had gotten involved in an opportunity to own his own business and planning his future as an entrepreneur. His commitment and resilience paid off because he got his business, left our carpool and the prison.

I mentioned earlier, middle-aged, and older officers had similar mannerisms including their sense of humor. One morning I rode shotgun which provided more elbow room than in the rear seat, which usually was three deep. At some point during the trip, Doug, the driver, asked if I had seen the woman in the vehicle which had passed us. I answered "no" because I was trying to sleep. I humored him by asking what about her. He responded he was sure she wanted him. I followed along, asking what made him so sure of her intentions. He replied, "watch this" and accelerated the old vehicle he was driving. As we passed the vehicle, he asked if I saw what she was doing. I commented her head was forward with both hands on the steering wheel. Doug agreed and assured me she wanted him, was playing hard to get, and wanted him to make the first move. While Doug had a serious expression and sounded convincing when he spoke, I knew he was joking (probably). This type of humor filled the trips to work every morning.

The trip home continued with joking as well as a case of beer meaning each of us consumed at least four beers in the forty-mile drive. Of course, none of us had to drink, but we agreed it would seem impolite not to share, and, besides, we were celebrating the fact there were no riots and each of us could go home after another day at work. While we were aware of the possible outcome of going to work each day, the group never discussed the reality.

The hall to my office opened to the same corridor as the cellblocks. I would routinely check in with the officers in the units. I was one of the employees who wore a tie to work which immediately put me in the category of not being a correctional officer. Consequently, while initially treated as an administrator, riding in the carpool made up of correctional officers as well as frequent visits to the units resulted in me becoming one of the 'good ol' boys' and the formality dissipated. Occasionally, the officer would offer a bad cup of coffee which I accepted. I reciprocated by sharing a candy bar or other snacks with the officers. Because I carried a small tablet in my shirt pocket, a clipboard with a tablet I got the reputation of authoring a book.

I had no intention during those years because events were happening too quickly to think about anything other than the day's crisis. To play along, I would occasionally pull the notebook out of my pocket, explain I was drafting a book and there would be a section devoted to the correctional staff. I told them I would title their portion of the book 'Words of wisdom from the trenches.' Each officer played along with me and gave me daily pearls of wisdom. One officer looked me straight in the eyes and proudly said, 'You go here, you go there, and there you are.' He then asked if I got his quote written down or if he needed to repeat it. I assured him I had written it exactly as he said and promised it would be in the book. I am not sure where the tablet is, but I will never forget those pearls of wisdom from the trenches. I can now say I kept my promise and put his words of wisdom in print. George, this was for you.

The nature of those incarcerated as well as those choosing to work in the prison setting created a unique environment which could not be duplicated in the basement of a psychology department. Having worked in four prisons, I knew the Stanford Prison Study had no relationship to reality. Recent findings support my observation it was not a good study because of coaching from faculty and other details not included in the original discussion.

In the 'real' world, staff and most inmates strive for homeostasis -- a balance to create a safe place to work as well as allow those convicted of a crime to complete their sentence and return to the community.

To Beard or Not to Beard

Before arriving at the facility, the Chief Psychologist at Marion encouraged me to shave my beard. The warden forbade facial hair on staff. Even after the Central Office approved beards, our warden stood his ground in stressing no beards. While he stood his ground, it took a special type of person coming to work every day and not knowing when or if they would go home which resulted in a standoff. Each of us had a bit of Maverick in us with twenty or thirty staff off the grid. The notion of not caring was useful on the job, but not when dealing with the warden.

The president of the union, a tremendous officer but outspoken, grew a beard and preempted the warden's preference. When the captain asked why he was going against the warden's request, he explained the Central Office had previously approved the policy. When other staff saw nothing happened to this brave, defiant officer, one-fourth of the staff grew beards.

Most staff did not approve of the facial hair, and I found it interesting to watch adult men stepping out of reality and into a Dr. Seuss book--the beards and the non-beards. While everyone got along, the non-bearded group viewed the bearded ones as not loyal to the facility. Something not explained to the staff was facial hair would interfere with a tight fit of a gas mask. While this concern was not an issue in less secure prisons, it could be more than a daily event where we worked. But administration and the bearded officers had been drawn in the sand with neither backing down.

One afternoon the warden shared a story with me regarding beards. While conquering the world, Julius Caesar would order his soldiers to polish their shields when not in combat or constructing roads. As the sun rose the morning before a battle, he would have the legends hold up their shields toward the rising sun. He could tell which centurions were the most loyal because their soldiers had the shiniest shields. Those units would be placed in the position where the most serious conflict might occur. The warden explained, the beard issue was like the shiny shields of Caesar's army, indicating the level of loyalty to the mission of the prison.

In any case, the beard and not-bearded discussions became a bore, and we moved forward. I am sure one of the riots contributed to dealing with other issues and some officers learning about the not-so-tight fit of the masks with facial hair.

Related situations

At times there were no local, regional, or national meetings, and the chief would be on campus. He regretted I could not attend the Warden's Meeting because, by my attendance, he could keep up with what was happening in the facility. I have not figured out how my attendance kept him in the loop because he never asked about the meetings, but I was glad to assist him.

My responsibilities were behind at least five grills, and I missed much happening in the administrative area. The chief was on the committee to interview applicants. One of the secretaries showed me documents in the trash which indicated my chief would remove certificates from the folders of applicants which he did not have in his personnel file, make a copy of the certificate, white out the name, put his name on the document, and place the copy in his folder.

I kept a three-ring binder of such situations, which proved useful in the following years. Like other organizations, a whistleblower (snitching in the area where I worked) was accepted but often with grave consequences to their career. I decided to wait until the right situation arose to avoid fallout from my binder.

While in the facility, he bombarded me with prattling about

his experience and conquests. Trying to find solace in the stall of a restroom did not help because he followed me and continued talking. Besides his not assisting in keeping the evaluations in the segregation units updated, my responsibility of the daily waking, and demeaning attitude toward me, I had gotten tired of his one-sided conversations.

One morning on my way to work, I concluded I could not stop his talking but could decide on the day's topic. For example, one topic I chose was breeding border collies. It was a coincidence his aunt in Jacksonville bred and sold registered border collies. My idea was working. My schedule included finding daily topics I would be interesting or entertaining. The chosen topics, presented as a question, led to his lengthy discourse on his expertise. He would start the conversation, which often lasted the eight-hour shift. The only way the discussion did not last was if someone else asked him a question regarding a different topic. The question became an immediate stimulus which resulted in his changing topics. Once, I shared my devious plan with a coworker who had great difficulty restraining himself from not laughing while listening to the on-going constant prattling.

CHAPTER 11

THE BEGINNING OF THE END

While at USP-Marion, I tried to respond to each situation in the best and most ethical manner I could. Some of my attempts were successful, while others not so much. Not every day was an adventure or even with stressors, but the cumulative effects of the years began to take its toll. I know many of the correctional staff had spent at least twice the time at the facility as I did, but I noticed a change in my attitude. While adapting to the situation, I was still sympathetic to the plight of some of those incarcerated at Marion.

On the other hand, I developed a deep disdain for predators. An example of a change in my ideas was my previous position concerning capital punishment. Over time my opinion became callused with the conviction predators would not change their inhumane, sadistic behavior regardless of where they were housed and needed to be permanently removed from society. Questions arising during those years included how many lives a person must take before society says, 'No More!'? Those who prey on others, such as the rapist/murderer from the United States Penitentiary in Atlanta, Georgia, should not have the luxury of remaining alive. However unacceptable Bill's, the executioner, logic was, one had to wonder what the correct way of handling similar crimes would be. Then, the reader must remember Bill was one of those taking lives.

Eight months after transferring to a different facility, the person who put a contract on my life killed one of the officers in the Control Unit. The rumor in Virginia was taking the officer's life was a show of power, demonstrating the organized group could kill anyone anywhere. The officer killed in the Control Unit was the fourth government employee who lost their life because of his violence. Why jeopardize the lives of others serving in maintaining peace in prisons? Prison officials assured he was transferred to a facility from which he would never be in a general population or pose a threat to others. Why did it take four victims before saying enough? It was because of him and similar situations which resulted in construction of the supermax. While I question the humaneness of such a facility, who can think of a better way to protect us from predators?

Those questions, and others, filled, and continue to occupy, my thoughts. While never involved, I had suited up to enter a unit to squash a riot. After suiting up and preparing to be involved in ending a riot, I questioned how valuable I remained considering my role in the system. At times, the role of a psychologist in prisons may be a delicate balance. In most situations, the line is obvious. At other times, there was a gray area where the correct, ethical decision was based on the answer of for whom I am working. Answers to 'for whom am I working' question included: the incarcerated individual; the agency in which I am employed; or the society in which I live. My original view was to protect those incarcerated and try to protect them from the chaos of the prison culture. As the years rolled by, my concern moved toward the safety of fellow staff. Also, the Parole Commission should never allow a small number of individuals to ever return to the 'free' world.

As I reframed those thoughts, I became more calloused. Not only at work but with staff in the carpool, my family, and non-prison friends whose number was small. The shift in values led to what I now see resulting in poor decision-making. Close to the end of my time, I grew frustrated. A major frustration was the person who was the director of the psychology department. My perceptions were, and continue to be, I was more responsible for any part of the decisions or essential work within the department. I completed paperwork, including the budget, while my last annual evaluation placed my overall rating in the average range. This disturbed me because my attitude and enthusiasm in my job were not average. The warden, down to the newest officer, supported my efforts.

One particularly bad, wintry day, contributing to my being overwhelmed with frustration, I made my way to the administrative section and asked a member of human services if I could review my job evaluation. It was legally available to me, and Carl handed me the form. I proceeded to tear it into small pieces of paper. While tearing the paper, the person in the office kept repeating I could not destroy the document. I told him I could. It was only paper. While not the wisest decision I ever made, it reflected my frustration.

The pieces of paper were handed to the director of human services, who presented them to the warden, who called the chief psychologist into his office. A call to the regional psychologist resulted in a visit from him the following week. He expressed his concern about my attitude as he showed me the evaluation which the chief had taped together. He was in the process of giving me three days off without pay allowing me the opportunity to think about my actions and future. I explained I had been requesting a transfer to the administrator with whom I was speaking for at least two years and telling him I was 'fried' and needed relief. I presented a three-ring binder of concerns I had collected over the years. The binder had documents implicating my supervisor in issues of ethical and legal concerns. I explained the original copies were in a similar binder at my home. If he decided to give me three days off, I assured him I would spend the first day sharing the binder with local and national news outlets. On the second day, I would find other employment and go fishing on the third day. I had played my shorthand correctly because I did not get the three days off.

However, I applied for and was offered a position in the Missouri state mental health system. I submitted my resignation immediately after the visit from the region psychologist. It must have been a coincidence, but I received a call during an evening a few days later and offered a pay raise if I transferred to a different federal prison. I accepted the opportunity because I learned I enjoyed the challenge of trying to make sense of and work in the hectic corrections system. Our country had created and perpetuated the system as the best answer for addressing incarcerating offenders. Our species had advanced in many ways, but those who did not fit in for one reason or another were subjected to removal in a system whose only rules were to house them until death or blood on a cell floor.

EPILOGUE

Each event described in these pages occurred. I leave the reader to form their own opinions regarding the events I described and how I managed those events. Unlike the other three prisons where I worked, the psychology department hall opened to the main corridor of the cell blocks. Psychology offices were not involved with the daily events of the units. The events in which I found myself would not occur if the situation was the case at Marion. While I had adequate supervision, circumstances were different and occurred quickly. I did my best to fulfill the expectations given to me.

The system changed me more than I was able to change the system. After watching my intentions and interactions, one of the regular visitors to my office told me I was the strange one who did not fit in. I considered his observation the highest compliment received during those years. Similar descriptions are the way psychologists should interact. This responsibility is not always easy while maintaining a delicate balance.

Were there regrets about leaving the prison system? Absolutely! Were there opportunities I would have never experienced or learned without leaving the prison system? Absolutely!

After all those years, I followed Yogi Berra's advice: "When you come to a fork in the road, take it."

ABOUT THE AUTHOR

Before resigning from the Federal Prison System, Doctor Kohutek worked in four prisons. The first assignment was the Federal Correctional Institution at Seagoville, TX. After six years at Marion, he transferred to the Federal Reformatory at Petersburg, Virginia and, finally, the Federal Correctional Institution at Texarkana, TX. His responsibilities included providing psychological services to those incarcerated at the prison camp attached to USP-Marion. While opportunities opened before and after resigning, he realized the length of time and experiences at Marion had changed him into a cynical person.

He took his experiences and started working with youthful offenders, high risk adolescents, and youth. He was co-owner of the Hazel Street Family Center in Texarkana, Texas. He maintained a private practice in conjunction with the center, was the clinical director of two residential treatment centers, and, eventually, became involved in the educational system. While a visiting professor at the University of Tampa, he developed a program to assist students in grades K-2 in planning, problem-solving, and memory. He retired from the field of mental health after years of working in elementary and secondary schools.